I0158380

THE WONDERFUL *LITRPG*

WIZARD OF OZ

By Oisin Muldowney

Based on the original text of L. Frank Baum

LEVEL UP
PUBLISHING

Published by Level Up in the United Kingdom in 2020

Cover image: Poko

ISBN: 978-1-83919-348-4

www.levelup.pub

ACKNOWLEDGEMENTS

To the memory of L. Frank Baum, obviously, for the original fantasy story. I hadn't read *The Wizard of Oz* since I was a teenager and was surprised how many battles there were and how much magic. It lends itself well to the LitRPG treatment.

Thanks also to my Second Life friends, Poko (who took the picture), Nina, and Sophie Awhā for posing for the cover with me.

CHAPTER I

The Cyclone

Dorothy was a level 1 Sorceress who lived in the midst of the great Kansas prairies with Uncle Henry, who was a level 0 NPC farmer, and Aunt Em, who was also an NPC, the farmer's wife. Their house was small, for the lumber to build it had to be carried by wagon many miles. There were four walls, a floor and a roof, which made one room; and this room contained a rusty looking cookstove, a cupboard for the dishes, a table, three or four chairs, and the beds. Uncle Henry and Aunt Em had a big bed in one corner, and Dorothy a little bed in another corner. There was no garret at all, and no cellar: except a small hole dug in the ground, called a cyclone cellar, where the family could go in case one of those great whirlwinds arose, mighty enough to crush any building in its path. It was reached by a trap door in the middle of the floor, from which a ladder led down into the small, dark hole.

When Dorothy stood in the doorway and looked around, she could see nothing but the ghostly traces of her UI and the great gray prairie on every side. Not a tree nor a house broke the broad sweep of flat country that reached to the edge of the sky in all directions. The sun had baked the plowed land into a gray mass,

1

with little cracks running through it. Even the grass was not green, for the sun had burned the tops of the long blades until they were the same gray color to be seen everywhere. Once the house had been painted, but the sun blistered the paint and the rains washed it away, and now the house was as dull and gray as everything else.

When Aunt Em came there to live she was a young, pretty wife with a Charisma of 15. The sun and wind had changed her, too. They had taken the sparkle from her eyes and left them a sober gray; they had taken the red from her cheeks and lips, and they were gray also. The Kansas landscape debuff of -1 Charisma per five years was probably not permanent but it might as well have been, for Aunt Em had nowhere else to go.

She was thin and gaunt, and never smiled now, reducing her Charisma to 9. When Dorothy, who was an orphan, first came to her, Aunt Em had been so startled by the child's laughter that she would scream and press her hand upon her heart whenever Dorothy's merry voice reached her ears; and she still looked at the little girl with wonder that she could find anything to laugh at.

Uncle Henry never laughed. He worked hard from morning till night and did not know what joy was. He was gray also, from his long beard to his rough boots, and he looked stern and solemn, and rarely spoke.

It was her familiar, Toto, who made Dorothy laugh, and saved her from growing as gray as her other surroundings. Toto was not gray; he was a little black dog, with long silky hair and small black eyes that twinkled merrily on either side of his funny, wee nose.

Toto played all day long, and Dorothy played with him, and loved him dearly.

Toto
Level 1 Familiar
HP 2
Dog form: Attacks 1 (bite), damage 1-2; AC 2 (+2 Dex) Brave (+4 on morale checks); Loyal (+4 on mind influencing checks); Magic Resistant (+4 on all saves vs. magical attacks)

Dorothy longed to progress as a Sorceress, but she was stuck on level 1. Her only spells were the *Detect Magic* and *Read Magic* that every magic-using class was granted at creation. And the farm didn't even have the usual Large Rat and Large Bat yardtrash that allowed new characters to gain experience. Instead, Toto scampered after imaginary foes and Dorothy pretended to assist him with *Magic Missile* and *Lightning Bolt*, as though she were a level 5 Sorceress. Her greatest dream was to actually own a copy of those spells in her spellbook.

Today, however, they were not playing. Uncle Henry sat upon the doorstep and looked anxiously at the sky, which was even grayer than usual. Dorothy stood in the door with Toto in her arms, and looked at the sky too. Aunt Em was washing the dishes.

From the far north they heard a low wail of the wind, and making her perception check, Dorothy could see where the long grass bowed in waves before the coming storm. There now came a sharp whistling in the air from the south, and as they turned their eyes that way they saw ripples in the grass coming from that direction also.

Suddenly, Uncle Henry stood up.

"There's a cyclone coming, Em," he called to his wife. "I'll go look after the stock." Then he ran toward the sheds where the cows and horses were kept.

Aunt Em dropped her work and came to the door. One glance told her of the danger close at hand.

"Quick, Dorothy!" she screamed. "Run for the cellar!"

Toto jumped out of Dorothy's arms and hid under the bed, and the girl started to get him. Aunt Em, badly frightened, threw open the trap door in the floor and climbed down the ladder into the small, dark hole. Dorothy caught Toto at last and started to follow her aunt. When she was halfway across the room there came a great shriek from the wind, and the house shook so hard that she lost her footing and sat down suddenly upon the floor.

Then a strange thing happened.

The house whirled around two or three times and rose slowly through the air. Dorothy felt as if she were going up in a balloon.

The north and south winds met where the house stood, and made it the exact center of the cyclone. In the middle of a cyclone the air is generally still, but the great pressure of the wind on every side of the house raised it up higher and higher, until it was at the very top of the cyclone; and there it remained and was carried miles and miles away as easily as you could carry a feather.

It was very dark, and the wind howled horribly around her, but Dorothy found she was riding quite easily. After the first few whirls around, and one other time when the house tipped badly, she felt as if she were being rocked gently, like a baby in a cradle.

Toto did not like it. He ran about the room, now here, now there, barking loudly; but Dorothy sat quite still on the floor and waited to see what would happen.

Once Toto got too near the open trap door, and fell in; and at first the little girl thought she had lost him. But soon she saw one of his ears sticking up through the hole, for the strong pressure of the air was keeping him up so that he could not fall. She crept to the hole, caught Toto by the ear, and dragged him into the room again, afterward closing the trap door so that no more accidents could happen.

Hour after hour passed away, and slowly Dorothy got over her fright; but she felt quite lonely, and the wind shrieked so loudly all about her that she nearly became deaf. For a time she had wondered if she would be dashed to pieces when the house fell again; but as the hours passed and nothing terrible happened, she stopped worrying and resolved to wait calmly and see what the future would bring. At last she crawled over the swaying floor to her bed, and lay down upon it; and Toto followed and lay down beside her.

In spite of the swaying of the house and the wailing of the wind, Dorothy soon closed her eyes and fell fast asleep.

CHAPTER II

The Council with the Munchkins

Dorothy was awakened by a shock, so sudden and severe that her 3 hit points were reduced to -3, and she should have been unconscious and in danger of dying. As it was, the jar made her catch her breath only. For it was followed by a most delightful series of seven chimes and a sense of health and power that she had never before experienced.

Lying there, wondering what had happened, Dorothy felt Toto put his cold little nose into her face and give a cheerful bark. A pop-up notice appeared:

> You have slain the Wicked Witch of the East!
>
> Exp gain 140,000.
>
> You are now level 8.
>
> You have 8 Attribute points to spend. You have 24 Skill points to spend.
>
> You have unlocked level 2 Spells.
>
> You have unlocked level 3 Spells.
>
> You have unlocked level 4 Spells.

```
You may now cast:

4 level 1 Spells

3 level 2 Spells

2 level 3 Spells

1 level 4 Spell
```

Confused by why she had gained so much experience, but thrilled by her rapid progress, Dorothy sat up and called up her character sheet.

```
Dorothy, level 8 Sorceress

HP 27   Mana 80

Str 5

Int 12

Wis 11

Con 5

Dex 6

Cha 13
```

Since a Sorceress cast Int-based spells, the obvious choice was to boost Intelligence, but Dorothy had been brought up by her uncle and aunt to appreciate that min-maxing was a foolish idea, because neglecting any Attribute too much had consequences. In her case, it was obvious that she needed more hit points, which came from allocating more points in Constitution. Dexterity wasn't too urgent, but there would be checks for activities such as leaping or climbing that would be penalized by only having a 6.

And the same for Strength. Her spend would therefore be 2 Str, 3 Int, 2 Con, 1 Dex.

Dorothy, level 8 Sorceress
HP 43   Mana 98
Str 7
Int 15
Wis 11
Con 7
Dex 7
Cha 13

Very satisfied with her new stats, Dorothy turned her attention to spells. There were now ten gem slots down the left side of her UI. Unfortunately, eight were grayed out. She simply didn't have the spells in her spell book to assign to them. The only active gems were the top two level 1 slots, where *Read Magic* and *Detect Magic* were assigned.

Dorothy closed the character sheet and noticed that the house was not moving; nor was it dark, for the bright sunshine came in at the window, flooding the little room. She sprang from her bed and with Toto at her heels ran and opened the door.

The little girl gave a cry of amazement and looked about her, her eyes growing bigger and bigger at the wonderful sights she saw.

The cyclone had set the house down very gently—for a cyclone—in the midst of a country of marvelous beauty. There were lovely patches of greensward all about, with stately trees bearing rich and luscious fruits. Banks of gorgeous flowers were on every hand, and birds with rare and brilliant plumage sang and fluttered in the trees and bushes. A little way off was a small brook, rushing and sparkling along between green banks, and murmuring in a voice very grateful to a little girl who had lived so long on the dry, gray prairies.

While she stood looking eagerly at the strange and beautiful sights, she noticed coming toward her a group of the queerest people she had ever seen. They were not as big as the grown folk she had always been used to; but neither were they very small. In fact, they seemed about as tall as Dorothy, who was a well-grown child for her age, although they were, so far as looks go, many years older. A quick check showed them all to be level 0 NPCs.

Three were men and one a woman, and all were oddly dressed. They wore round hats that rose to a small point a foot above their heads, with little bells around the brims that tinkled sweetly as they moved. The hats of the men were blue; the little woman's hat was white, and she wore a white gown that hung in pleats from her shoulders. Over it were sprinkled little stars that glistened in the sun like diamonds. The men were dressed in blue, of the same shade as their hats, and wore well-polished boots with a deep roll of blue at the tops. The men, Dorothy thought, were about as old as Uncle Henry, for two of them had beards. But the little woman was doubtless much older. Her face was covered with wrinkles, her hair was nearly white, and she walked rather stiffly.

When these people drew near the house where Dorothy was standing in the doorway, they paused and whispered among themselves, as if afraid to come farther. But the little old woman walked up to Dorothy, made a low bow and said, in a sweet voice:

"You are welcome, most noble Sorceress, to the land of the Munchkins. We are so grateful to you for having killed the Wicked Witch of the East, and for setting our people free from bondage."

Dorothy listened to this speech with wonder. True, she had seen the message that she had killed the Wicked Witch of the East, but how had she done that? She had no offensive spells and no recollection of casting any, or of little Toto attacking with his minor bite.

The little woman evidently expected her to answer; so Dorothy said, with hesitation, "You are very kind, but there must be some mistake. I have not killed anything."

"Your house did, anyway," replied the little old woman, with a laugh, "and that is the same thing. See!" she continued, pointing to the corner of the house. "There are her two feet, still sticking out from under a block of wood."

Dorothy looked, and gave a little cry of delight. There, indeed, just under the corner of the great beam the house rested on, two feet were sticking out, shod in silver shoes with pointed toes.

"Oh, what luck! What luck!" cried Dorothy, laughing. "The house must have fallen on her. That explains the way I could win a boss fight, even though I was only level one and with no useful spells."

"Congratulations," said the little woman calmly.

"But what level was she?" asked Dorothy.

"She was a level ten Witch," answered the little woman. "She has held all the Munchkins in bondage for many years, making them slave for her night and day. Now they are all set free, and are grateful to you for the favor."

"Who are the Munchkins?" inquired Dorothy.

"They are the people who live in this land of the East where the Wicked Witch ruled."

"Are you a Munchkin?" asked Dorothy.

"No, but I am their friend, although I live in the land of the North. When they saw the Witch of the East was dead the Munchkins sent a swift messenger to me, and I came at once. I am the Witch of the North."

"Oh, gracious!" cried Dorothy. "A Witch; can you teach me some spells?"

"Yes, indeed," answered the little woman. "But I am only level five, nowhere near as powerful as the Wicked Witch was who ruled here, or I should have set the people free myself."

"What's in your spellbook?" asked the girl, who could only think of one thing: that she might soon achieve her ambition of being able to cast *Magic Missile* and *Lightning Bolt*.

"We'll come to that. First, you should know there were only four Witches of level five and above in all the Land of Oz, and two of them, those who live in the North and the South, are good witches. I know this is true, for I am one of them myself, and cannot be mistaken. Those who dwelt in the East and the West were, indeed, wicked witches; but now that you have killed one of them, there is but one Wicked Witch in all the Land of Oz—the one who lives in the West. And she also is level ten."

"I see," said Dorothy, after a moment's thought. "Yet Aunt Em has told me that the highest-level Witch in Kansas is only six."

"Who is Aunt Em?" inquired the little old woman.

"She is my aunt who lives in Kansas, where I came from."

The Witch of the North seemed to think for a time, with her head bowed and her eyes upon the ground. Then she looked up and said, "I do not know where Kansas is, for I have never heard that country mentioned before. But tell me, is it a *Pathfinder*-based RPG country?"

"Oh, yes," replied Dorothy.

"Then that accounts for it. In *Pathfinder*-based countries I believe levelling up is really difficult. But, you see, the Land of Oz has never been based on *Pathfinder*, for we are cut off from all the rest of the world. Therefore our laws are those of *Runescape*, with much higher level characters."

"Who is the highest-level character here?" asked Dorothy.

"Oz himself is the Great Wizard," answered the Witch, sinking her voice to a whisper. "He is more powerful than all the rest

13

of us together. He is level fifteen and lives in the City of Emeralds."

Dorothy was going to ask another question, but just then the Munchkins, who had been standing silently by, gave a loud shout and pointed to the corner of the house where the Wicked Witch had been lying.

"What is it?" asked the little old woman, and looked, and began to laugh. The feet of the dead Witch had disappeared entirely, and nothing was left but the silver shoes.

"She was dead six minutes," explained the Witch of the North, "dead mobs despawn after that time and can't be *Raised* or *Resurrected*. That is the end of her. But the Silver Shoes are yours, and you shall have them to wear." She reached down and picked up the shoes, and after shaking the dust out of them handed them to Dorothy.

"The Witch of the East was proud of those Silver Shoes," said one of the Munchkins, "it's her rare drop and there is some charm connected with them; but what it is we never knew."

Dorothy carried the shoes into the house and placed them on the table. Then she came out again to the Munchkins and said: "I am anxious to get back to my aunt and uncle, for I am sure they will worry about me. Can you help me find my way?"

The Munchkins and the Witch first looked at one another, and then at Dorothy, and then shook their heads.

"At the East, not far from here," said one, "there is a great desert, and none could live to cross it."

"It is the same at the South," said another, "for I have been there and seen it. The South is the country of the Quadlings."

"I am told," said the third man, "that it is the same at the West. And that country, where the Winkies live, is ruled by the Wicked Witch of the West, who would make you her slave if you passed her way."

"The North is my home," said the old lady, "and at its edge is the same great desert that surrounds this Land of Oz. I'm afraid, my dear, you will have to live with us."

Dorothy began to sob at this, for she felt lonely among all these strange people. Her tears seemed to grieve the kind-hearted Munchkins, for they immediately took out their handkerchiefs and began to weep also. As for the little old woman, she took off her cap and balanced the point on the end of her nose, while she counted "One, two, three" in a solemn voice. At once the cap changed to a slate, on which was written in big white chalk marks:

"LET DOROTHY GO TO THE CITY OF EMERALDS"

The little old woman took the slate from her nose, and having read the words of the *Cap of Augury*, asked, "Is your name Dorothy, my dear?"

"Yes," answered the child, looking up and drying her tears.

"Then you must go to the City of Emeralds. Perhaps Oz will help you."

"Where is this city?" asked Dorothy.

"It is exactly in the center of the country, and is ruled by Oz, the Great Wizard I told you of."

15

"Is he a good man?" inquired the girl anxiously.

"He is a good Wizard. Whether he is a man or not I cannot tell, for I have never seen him."

"How can I get there?" asked Dorothy.

"You must walk. It is a long journey, through a country that is sometimes pleasant and sometimes dark and terrible. However, I will use all the magic arts I know of to keep you from harm."

"Won't you go with me?" pleaded the girl, who had begun to look upon the little old woman as her only friend. "I need your spells."

"No, I cannot do that," she replied, "but I will give you three spells for your spellbook and I shall use up my *Limited Wish* that I have been saving for decades, ever since I completed the China Princess quest as a young Witch."

She came close to Dorothy and kissed her gently on the forehead. Where her lips touched the girl they left a round, shining mark, as Dorothy found out soon after.

"There. You now have a *Protection from Evil*, which will last for a month. The road to the City of Emeralds is paved with yellow brick," said the Witch, "so you cannot miss it. When you get to Oz do not be afraid of him, but tell your story and ask him to help you. Good-bye, my dear."

The three Munchkins bowed low to her and wished her a pleasant journey, after which they walked away through the trees. The Witch gave Dorothy a friendly little nod, whirled around on her left heel three times, and straightway disappeared, much to the surprise of little Toto, who barked after her loudly enough when she had gone, because he had been afraid even to growl while she stood by.

But Dorothy, knowing her to be a Witch with a *Dimension Door* spell, had expected her to disappear in just that way, and was not surprised in the least. Opening up her inventory, she was glad to see the kind Witch had given her the three spells as promised. These could be inscribed into her blank spell book.

While Toto ran around sniffing eagerly at all the new and strange flowers, Dorothy sat and mediated, dragging the icons to the first empty slots.

Magic Missile

Mana cost 12. Cast time 1 second. Refresh time 2 seconds.

Damages creatures vulnerable to magical energy attacks in proportion to the caster's level.

Stinking Cloud

Mana cost 24. Cast time 5 seconds. Refresh time 8 seconds.

Creates a sphere of noxious gas 20 yards in radius, at any point up to 100 yards from the caster, lasting 90 seconds per caster level. Creatures that breathe and who fail a fortitude check fall Nauseated for the

> duration. Those who succeed in their fortitude check
> must leave the cloud before taking any other action.

> ### Haste
>
> Mana cost 48. Cast time 8 seconds. Refresh time 24 seconds.
>
> All grouped allies within twenty yards of the caster receive the Haste buff for 1 minute per caster level. Movement +20%, attack speed +20%, AC+1.

Her HUD had spell gems for all of the slots she had unlocked: four first, three second, two third and one fourth. There were no hard choices to be made, no choices at all: Dorothy filled her gems with all her spells (*Read Magic, Detect Magic, Magic Missile, Stinking Cloud* and *Haste*), which still left her with grayed out gems for a first level spell, two second, one third and one fourth.

It was delightful to have more spells than simply *Read Magic* and *Detect Magic*. Yet Dorothy couldn't help but feel a twinge of regret that the Witch wasn't able to give her *Lightning Bolt* or *Fireball*. And what about a fourth level spell? *O my!* Dorothy thought. *Imagine being able to cast a fourth level spell; I never thought such a day would come.*

CHAPTER III

How Dorothy Saved the Scarecrow

When Dorothy was left alone she began to feel hungry. So she went to the cupboard and cut herself some bread, which she spread with butter. She gave some to Toto, and taking a pail from the shelf she carried it down to the little brook and filled it with clear, sparkling water. Toto ran over to the trees and began to bark at the birds sitting there. Dorothy went to get him, and saw such delicious fruit hanging from the branches that she gathered some of it, finding it just what she wanted to help out her breakfast.

Toto seemed more energetic than ever and out of curiosity, Dorothy checked the stats on her familiar:

Toto
HP 12
Level 5 Familiar
Dog form: Attacks 1 (bite), damage 9-16, AC 2 (+2 Dex)
Brave (+6 on morale checks); Loyal (+6 on mind influencing checks); Magic Resistant (+6 on all saves vs. magical attacks)

"Why Toto dear," said Dorothy, "you've levelled up handsomely too. That bite could come in very useful. And although your armor class and hit points are very low, you might just be able to delay a mob long enough for me to get a spell off."

Then she went back to the house, and having helped herself and Toto to a good drink of the cool, clear water, she set about making ready for the journey to the City of Emeralds.

Dorothy had only one other dress, but that happened to be clean and was hanging on a peg beside her bed. It was gingham, with checks of white and blue; and although the blue was somewhat faded with many washings, it was still a pretty frock. Unfortunately, it provided no bonus to armor class and Dorothy was conscious that she was AC 0, the worst possible in the game.

The girl washed herself carefully, dressed herself in the clean gingham, and tied her pink sunbonnet on her head. She took a little basket and filled it with bread from the cupboard, laying a white cloth over the top. Then she looked down at her feet and noticed how old and worn her shoes were.

"They surely will never do for a long journey, Toto," she said. And Toto looked up into her face with his little black eyes and wagged his tail to show he knew what she meant, which of course he did, since Sorceresses and their familiars had a *Telepathic Bond*.

At that moment Dorothy saw lying on the table the Silver Shoes that had belonged to the Witch of the East.

"I wonder if they are useable by the Sorceress class," she said to Toto. "Even without any magical bonus to my armor class they would be just the thing to take a long walk in, for they could not wear out."

She picked them up.

Silver Shoes of Proicio
Attune?
YES / NO

Of course, Dorothy chose to attune the Silver Shoes to her. With that, they became No Trade and no matter even if she were killed, it meant that the shoes could not be worn by anyone else. As Dorothy knew well from instruction by Uncle Henry, attunement discouraged player characters from killing one another for gear.

Dorothy took off her old leather shoes and tried on the silver ones, which fitted her as well as if they had been made for her. But whatever magical powers they had, she could not make out, despite trying all sorts of leaps and skips and jumps. Her armor class remained resolutely at 0.

"Am I faster perhaps?" she asked Toto, while running back and forth.

Toto did not seem impressed.

Finally, Dorothy picked up her basket. "Come along, Toto," she said. "We will go to the Emerald City and ask the Great Oz how to get back to Kansas again."

She closed the door, locked it, and put the key carefully in the pocket of her dress. And so, with Toto trotting along soberly behind her, she started on her journey.

There were several roads nearby, but it did not take her long to find the one paved with yellow bricks. Within a short time she was walking briskly toward the Emerald City, her Silver Shoes tinkling merrily on the hard, yellow road-bed. The sun shone bright and the birds sang sweetly, and Dorothy did not feel nearly so bad as you might think a little girl would who had been suddenly whisked away from her own country and set down in the midst of a strange land.

She was surprised, as she walked along, to see how pretty the country was about her. There were neat fences at the sides of the road, painted a dainty blue color, and beyond them were fields of grain and vegetables in abundance. Evidently the Munchkins were good farmers and able to raise large crops. Once in a while she would pass a house, and the people came out to look at her and bow low as she went by; for everyone knew she had been the means of destroying the Wicked Witch and setting them free from bondage. The houses of the Munchkins were odd-looking dwellings, for each was round, with a big dome for a roof. All were painted blue, for in this country of the East blue was the favorite color.

Toward evening, when Dorothy was tired with her long walk and began to wonder where she should pass the night, she came to a house rather larger than the rest. On the green lawn before it many men and women were dancing. Five little fiddlers played as loudly as possible, and the people were laughing and singing, while a big table nearby was loaded with delicious fruits and nuts, pies and cakes, and many other good things to eat.

The people greeted Dorothy kindly, and invited her to supper and to pass the night with them; for this was the home of one of the richest Munchkins in the land, and his friends were gathered with him to celebrate their freedom from the bondage of the Wicked Witch.

Dorothy ate a hearty supper and was waited upon by the rich Munchkin himself, whose name was Boq. Then she sat upon a settee and watched the people dance.

When Boq saw her Silver Shoes he said, "You must be a great Sorceress."

"Why?" asked the girl.

"Because you wear Silver Shoes and have killed the Wicked Witch. Besides, you have white in your frock, and only Witches and Sorceresses wear white."

"My dress is blue-and-white checked," said Dorothy, smoothing out the wrinkles in it.

"It is kind of you to wear that," said Boq. "Blue is the color of the Munchkins, and white is a sign of goodness. So we know you are a friendly Sorceress."

Dorothy did not know what to say to this, for in truth she was closer to Lawful Neutral than Lawful Good. Moreover, while all the people seemed to think her a powerful character, she knew very well she was only level 8 by an exploit. All her skills were unpracticed and therefore low and she had only three offensive spells. Even her *Restore Mana* skill was only at 5, meaning her mana pool would replenish at just 1 tick every 3 seconds. She was far from being the mighty Sorceress that her level suggested.

When she had tired watching the dancing, Boq led her into the house, where he gave her a room with a pretty bed in it. The sheets were made of blue cloth, and Dorothy spent most of the night casting *Detect Magic* with Toto curled up on the blue rug beside her. Not long before dawn, she had maxed her *Restore Mana* skill at 40, which gave her 11 ticks per second.

She ate a hearty breakfast, and watched a wee Munchkin baby, who played with Toto and pulled his tail and crowed and laughed in a way that greatly amused Dorothy. Toto was a fine curiosity to all the people, for they had never seen a dog familiar before.

"How far is it to the Emerald City?" Dorothy asked.

"I do not know," answered Boq gravely, "for I have never been there. It is better for people to keep away from Oz, unless they have business with him. But it is a long way to the Emerald City, and it will take you many days. The country here is rich and pleasant, but you must pass through rough and dangerous places with high chances of wandering monsters before you reach the end of your journey."

This worried Dorothy a little, but she knew that only the Great Oz could help her get to Kansas again, so she bravely resolved not to turn back.

She bade her friends good-bye, and again started along the road of yellow brick. When she had gone several miles she thought she would stop to rest, and so climbed to the top of the fence beside the road and sat down. There was a great cornfield beyond the fence, and not far away she saw a Scarecrow, placed high on a pole to keep the birds from the ripe corn.

Dorothy leaned her chin upon her hand and gazed thoughtfully at the Scarecrow. Its head was a small sack stuffed with straw, with eyes, nose, and mouth painted on it to represent a face. An old, pointed blue hat, that had belonged to some Munchkin, was perched on his head, and the rest of the figure was a blue suit of clothes, worn and faded, which had also been stuffed with straw. On the feet were some old boots with blue tops, such as every man wore in this country, and the figure was raised above the stalks of corn by means of the pole stuck up its back.

While Dorothy was looking earnestly into the queer, painted face of the Scarecrow, she was surprised to see one of the eyes slowly wink at her. She thought she must have been mistaken at first, for none of the scarecrows in Kansas ever wink, even straw golems; but presently the figure nodded its head to her in a friendly way. Then she climbed down from the fence and walked up to it, while Toto ran around the pole and barked.

"Good day," said the Scarecrow, in a rather husky voice.

"Did you speak?" asked the girl, in wonder.

"Certainly," answered the Scarecrow. "How do you do?"

"I'm pretty well, thank you," replied Dorothy politely. "How do you do?"

"I'm not feeling well," said the Scarecrow, with a smile, "for it is very tedious being perched up here night and day to scare away giant rats."

"Can't you get down?" asked Dorothy.

"No, for I have been tightly fastened to this pole up my back. If you will please take away the pole I shall be greatly obliged to you."

Dorothy reached up both arms and attempted to lift the figure off the pole, thinking that being stuffed with straw, he would be quite light. The ropes around the Scarecrow, however, had been tied very tightly indeed.

Stepping back, Dorothy pointed at the biggest knots and cast *Magic Missile*. On the third bolt, the ropes broke apart and the Scarecrow fell down.

"Thank you very much," said the Scarecrow, when he had lifted himself to his feet. "I feel like a new man."

Dorothy was puzzled at this, for it sounded queer to hear a stuffed man speak, and to see him bow and walk along beside her.

"Who are you?" asked the Scarecrow when he had stretched himself and yawned. "And where are you going?"

"My name is Dorothy," said the girl, "and I am going to the Emerald City, to ask the Great Oz to send me back to Kansas."

"Where is the Emerald City?" he inquired. "And who is Oz?"

"Why, don't you know?" she returned, in surprise.

"No, indeed. I don't know anything. You see, I was a human Bard, before I got hit by a *Curse* by the Wicked Witch of the East when my Intelligence was only six, so I have no brains left at all," he answered sadly. "And I was *Polymorphed* into a straw man and left to serve her minions as a lesson."

"Oh," said Dorothy, "I'm awfully sorry for you."

"Do you think," he asked, "if I go to the Emerald City with you, that Oz would cast *Dispel Magic* on the *Curse* and *Polymorph* and restore my race and Intelligence?"

"I cannot tell," she returned, "but you may come with me, if you like. If Oz will not remove the *Curse*, you will be no worse off than you are now."

"That is true," said the Scarecrow. "You see," he continued confidentially, "I might not revert to human. I don't mind my legs and arms and body being stuffed, because I cannot get hurt. If anyone smashes a mace on my toes or sticks a sword into me, it doesn't matter, for it only does one point of damage. But I do want my Bard abilities back, and if my Intelligence stays on zero, how am I ever to give performances or cast spells again? Not to mention the penalties on my skills make most of them useless."

"I understand how you feel," said the little girl, who was truly sorry for him. "If you will come with me I'll ask Oz to do all he can for you."

"Thank you," he answered gratefully. "Shall we form a group? Although I'm a level seven Bard, I am not much use with a zero intelligence but perhaps even my small contribution will help you."

27

"Certainly," said Dorothy and she sent the invitation from her UI, which the Scarecrow promptly accepted.

They walked back to the road. Dorothy helped him over the fence, and they started along the path of yellow brick for the Emerald City.

Toto did not like this addition to the party at first. He smelled around the stuffed man as if he suspected there might be a nest of rats in the straw, and he often growled in an unfriendly way at the Scarecrow.

"Don't mind Toto," said Dorothy to her new friend. "He only bites when I command him to."

"Oh, I'm not afraid," replied the Scarecrow. "He can't hurt the straw. Do let me carry that basket for you. I shall not mind it, for I can't get tired. I'll tell you a secret," he continued, as he walked along. "There is only one thing in the world I am afraid of."

"What is that?" asked Dorothy; "the Witch who *Cursed* and *Polymorphed* you? Because if so, I have some good news for you."

"No," answered the Scarecrow; "it's a lighted match."

CHAPTER IV

The Road Through the Forest

After a few hours the road began to be rough, and the walking grew so difficult that the Scarecrow often stumbled over the yellow bricks, which were very uneven. Sometimes, indeed, they were broken or missing altogether, leaving holes that Toto jumped across and Dorothy walked around. As for the Scarecrow, having 0 Intelligence, he walked straight ahead, and so stepped into the holes and fell at full length on the hard bricks. It never hurt him, however, and Dorothy would pick him up and set him upon his feet again, while he joined her in laughing merrily at his own mishap.

The farms were not nearly so well cared for here as they were farther back. There were fewer houses and fewer fruit trees, and the farther they went the more dismal and lonesome the country became.

At noon they sat down by the roadside, near a little brook, and Dorothy opened her basket and got out some bread. She offered a piece to the Scarecrow, but he refused.

"I am never hungry," he said, "and it is a lucky thing I am not, for my mouth is only painted, and if I should cut a hole in it so I could eat, the straw I am stuffed with would come out, and that would spoil the shape of my head."

Dorothy saw at once that this was true, so she only nodded and went on eating her bread.

"Tell me something about yourself and the country you came from," said the Scarecrow, when she had finished her dinner. So she told him all about Kansas, and how gray everything was there, so gray that it was a gradual Charisma debuff, and how she had just been a level 1 Sorceress with no useful spells and no hope of levelling up until the cyclone had carried her to this queer Land of Oz.

The Scarecrow listened carefully, and said, "I cannot understand why you should wish to leave this beautiful country where you have a much better chance of levelling up—not to mention magic and treasure—and go back to the dry, gray place you call Kansas, which doesn't even have a giant rat for you to blow up."

"That is because you have forgotten what it was like to be human," answered the girl. "No matter how dreary and gray our homes are, we people of flesh and blood would rather live there than in any other country, be it ever so beautiful. There is no place like home. Moreover, if I can return home an eighth level Sorceress, I will be the highest level Int-based caster in the state."

The Scarecrow sighed.

"Of course I cannot understand it," he said. "If you were all *Polymorphed*, like me, you would probably all go to live in beautiful places, and then Kansas would have no people at all. It is fortunate for Kansas that you remain human."

"Won't you entertain me with a Bardic epic, while we are resting?" asked the child.

The Scarecrow looked at her reproachfully, and answered:

"My life has been so upended that I really know nothing whatever of my previous repertoire. I was only *Cursed* the day before yesterday. What happened before that time is all a blur. I only know I was a human Bard from the grayed-out abilities on my UI. Unluckily, after the Witch *Polymorphed* me into a figure of straw I was found by a Lawful Evil farmer who reckoned I would be perfect for warding off the giant rats who raided his crops.

"He began by painting my ears, so that I heard what was going on. There was another of the Witch's minions with him, and the first thing I heard was the farmer saying, 'How do you like those ears?'

"'They aren't straight,' answered the other.

"'Never mind,' said the farmer. 'They are ears just the same and he will be able to hear the rats,' which was true enough.

"'Now I'll make the eyes,' said the farmer. So he painted my right eye, and as soon as it was finished I found myself looking at him and at everything around me with a great deal of curiosity, for this felt like my first glimpse of the world.

"'That's not a very frightening eye,' remarked the minion who was watching the farmer. 'Blue paint is too cheerful for scary eyes.'

31

"'I think I'll make the other a little bigger,' said the farmer. And when the second eye was done I could see much better than before. Then he made my nose and my mouth so I could shout at the rats. But I did not speak, because at that time I had forgotten what a mouth was for. I had the fun of watching them tie my body and my arms and legs nice and tight; and when they secured my head, at last, I felt very proud, for I thought I was just as good a character as anyone.

"'This fellow will scare the rats fast enough,' said the farmer. 'And crows too, he looks just like a PC.'

"'Why, he was a PC,' said the other, and I quite agreed with him, because I could see my UI, even if most of the action buttons were grayed out. The farmer carried me under his arm to the cornfield, and tied me tight to a tall stick, where you found me. He and his friend soon after walked away and left me alone.

"I did not like to be constrained in this way. So I tried to escape. But my feet would not touch the ground, my Escape Artist skill was negative as a result of my zero Intelligence and that penalty for being suspended. I was forced to stay on that pole. It was a lonely life to lead, for I had nothing to think of, having been made such a little while before. Many crows and other birds flew into the cornfield, but as soon as they saw me they flew away again, thinking I was a Munchkin; and I found I could shout at giant rats, causing them to run away. This pleased me and made me hope I could perhaps gain XP, even by tiny increments, or as a reward for a quest fulfilled. But by and by an old crow flew near me, and after looking at me carefully he perched upon my shoulder and said:

"'I wonder if that farmer thought to fool me in this clumsy manner. Any crow of sense could see that you are only a prisoner stuffed with straw.' Then he hopped down at my feet and ate all the corn he wanted. The other birds, seeing he was not harmed by me, came to eat the corn too, so in a short time there was a great flock of them about me.

"I felt sad at this, for it showed I had no hope of advancing a level after all; but the old crow comforted me, saying, 'If you only had your Intelligence restored, you would be as good a PC as any of them, and a better character than some of them. A high Intelligence is the only thing worth having in this world, no matter whether one is a crow or a man. Not only does it increase your mana pool, if you are an Int-based caster, but it gives you faster skill increases.'

"After the crows had gone I thought this over, and decided I would try hard to get my Intelligence back and perhaps my human race too, although an animated straw-man Bard might be an awesome race and class combination: at least in respect to avoiding damage from blunt weapons, stabs and from falling. By good luck you came along and rescued me from the stake, and from what you say I am sure the Great Oz will lift the *Curse* as soon as we get to the Emerald City."

"I hope so," said Dorothy earnestly, "since you seem anxious to resume your chance of progressing as a Bard."

"Oh, yes; I am anxious," returned the Scarecrow. "It is such an uncomfortable feeling to know one is unable to use the abilities one has unlocked."

"Well," said the girl, "let us go." And she handed the basket to the Scarecrow.

There were no fences at all by the roadside now, and the land was rough and untilled. Toward evening they came to a great forest, where the trees grew so big and close together that their branches met over the road of yellow brick. It was almost dark under the trees, for the branches shut out the daylight; but the travelers did not stop, and went on into the forest.

"If this road goes in, it must come out," said the Scarecrow, "and as the Emerald City is at the other end of the road, we must go wherever it leads us."

"Anyone would know that," said Dorothy.

"Certainly; that is why I know it," returned the Scarecrow. "If it required Intelligence to figure it out, I never should have said it."

After an hour or so the light faded away, and they found themselves stumbling along in the darkness. Dorothy could not see at all, but Toto could, for some dogs see very well in the dark; and the Scarecrow declared he could see as well as by day. So she took hold of his arm and managed to get along fairly well.

"If you see any house, or any place where we can pass the night," she said, "you must tell me; for it is very uncomfortable walking in the dark."

Soon after the Scarecrow stopped.

"I see a little cottage at the right of us," he said, "built of logs and branches. Shall we go there?"

"Yes, indeed," answered the child. "I am all tired out."

The Scarecrow led her through the trees until they reached the cottage, and Dorothy entered and found a bed of dried leaves in one corner. She lay down at once, and with Toto beside her soon fell into a sound sleep. The Scarecrow, who was never tired, stood up in another corner and waited patiently until morning came.

CHAPTER V

The Rescue of the Tin Woman

When Dorothy awoke the sun was shining through the trees and Toto had long been out chasing birds around him and squirrels: the XP gain when he was successful was tiny, but all progress was worthwhile. She sat up and looked around her. There was the Scarecrow, still standing patiently in his corner, waiting for her.

"We must go and search for water," she said to him.

"Why do you want water?" he asked.

"To wash my face clean after the dust of the road, and to drink, so the dry bread will not stick in my throat."

"It must be inconvenient to be made of flesh," said the Scarecrow thoughtfully, "for you must sleep, and eat and drink. However, you have Intelligence above zero, and it is worth a lot of bother to be able to think properly."

They left the cottage and walked through the trees until they found a little spring of clear water, where Dorothy drank and bathed and ate her breakfast. She saw there was not much bread left in the basket, and the girl was thankful the Scarecrow did not have to eat anything, for there was scarcely enough for herself and Toto for the day.

When she had finished her meal, and was about to go back to the road of yellow brick, she was startled to hear a deep groan nearby.

"What was that?" she asked timidly.

"I cannot imagine," replied the Scarecrow; "but we can go and see. If it is alive, it might give us XP to kill it."

Just then another groan reached their ears, and the sound seemed to come from behind them. They turned and walked through the forest a few steps, when Dorothy discovered something shining in a ray of sunshine that fell between the trees. She ran to the place and then stopped short, with a little cry of surprise.

One of the big trees had been partly chopped through, and standing beside it, with an uplifted axe in her hands, was a woman made entirely of tin. Her head and arms and legs were jointed upon her body, but she stood perfectly motionless, as if she could not stir at all.

Dorothy looked at her in amazement, and so did the Scarecrow, while Toto barked sharply and made a snap at the tin legs, which hurt his teeth.

"Did you groan?" asked Dorothy.

"Yes," answered the Tin Woman, "I did. I've been groaning for more than a year, and no one has ever heard me before or come to help me."

"What can I do for you?" Dorothy inquired softly, for she was moved by the sad voice in which the woman spoke.

"Get an oil-can and oil my joints," she answered. "They are rusted so badly that I cannot move them at all; if I am well oiled I shall soon be all right again. You will find an oil-can on a shelf in my cottage."

Dorothy at once ran back to the cottage and found the oil-can, and then she returned and asked anxiously, "Where are your joints?"

"Oil my neck, first," replied the Tin Woman. So Dorothy oiled it, and as it was quite badly rusted the Scarecrow took hold of the tin head and moved it gently from side to side until it worked freely, and then the woman could turn it herself.

"Now oil the joints in my arms," she said. And Dorothy oiled them and the Scarecrow bent them carefully until they were quite free from rust and as good as new.

The Tin Woman gave a sigh of satisfaction and lowered her axe, which she leaned against the tree.

"This is a great comfort," she said. "I have been holding that axe in the air ever since I rusted, and I'm glad to be able to put it down at last. Now, if you will oil the joints of my legs, I shall be all right once more."

So they oiled her legs until she could move them freely; and she thanked them again and again for her release, for she seemed a very polite creature, and very grateful.

"I might have stood there always if you had not come along," she said; "so you have certainly saved my life. How did you happen to be here?"

"We are on our way to the Emerald City to see the Great Oz," Dorothy answered, "and we stopped at your cottage to pass the night."

"Why do you wish to see Oz?" the Tin Woman asked.

"I want him to send me back to Kansas, and the Scarecrow wants him to restore his Intelligence to six," she replied.

The Tin Woman appeared to think deeply for a moment. Then she said:

"Do you suppose Oz could provide an *Atonement* for me?"

"Why, I can't be sure," Dorothy answered. "*Atonement* is a divine spell and the Wizard is an arcane spell caster. But he might have powerful friends."

"True," the Tin Woman returned. "So, if you will allow me to join your party, I will also go to the Emerald City and ask Oz to help me."

"Come along," said the Scarecrow heartily, and Dorothy sent a group invite from her UI, adding that she would be pleased to have her company. So the Tin Woman shouldered her axe and they all passed through the forest until they came to the road that was paved with yellow brick.

The Tin Woman had asked Dorothy to put the oil-can in her basket. "For," she said, "if I should get caught in the rain, and rust again, I would need the oil-can badly."

It was a bit of good luck to have their new comrade join the party, for soon after they had begun their journey again they came to a place where the trees and branches grew so thick over the road that the travelers could not pass. But the Tin Woman set to work with her axe and chopped so well that soon she cleared a passage for the entire party.

Dorothy was thinking so earnestly as they walked along that she did not notice when the Scarecrow stumbled into a hole and rolled over to the side of the road. Indeed he was obliged to call to her to help him up again.

"Why didn't you walk around the hole?" asked the Tin Woman.

"I don't know enough," replied the Scarecrow cheerfully. "My head is stuffed with straw, you know, and that is why I am going to Oz to ask him for some Intelligence."

"Oh, I see," said the Tin Woman. "But, after all, Intelligence is not the best attribute in the world."

"Have you a high Intelligence?" inquired the Scarecrow.

"No, my head is quite empty, it's only five," answered the Tin Woman. "But I have a Constitution of seventeen; and I'm quite convinced that's the better stat to raise for me."

"And why is that?" asked the Scarecrow.

"I will tell you my story, and then you will know."

So, while they were walking through the forest, the Tin Woman told the following story:

"I was born human, the daughter of a woodman who chopped down trees in the forest and sold the wood for a living. When I grew up, I became a level one Paladin, and after my father died I took care of my old mother as long as she lived. Then I made up my mind that instead of living alone I would marry, so that I might not become lonely.

"There was one of the Munchkin boys who was so beautiful that I soon grew to love him with all my heart. He, on his part, promised to marry me as soon as I reached level five and unlocked *Angelic Aspect*; so I set to levelling up harder than ever. But the boy lived with an old woman who did not want him to marry anyone, for she was so lazy she wished the boy to remain with her and do the cooking and the housework. So the old woman went to the Wicked Witch of the East, and promised her two sheep and a cow if she would prevent the marriage. Thereupon the Wicked Witch enchanted my axe with *Malice*, and when I was grinding away at a goblin camp one day, for I was anxious to get the new house and my husband as soon as possible, the axe slipped all at once and cut off my left leg.

"This at first seemed a great misfortune, for I knew a one-legged woman could not do very well as a Paladin. So I went to a grandmaster gnomish Tinkerer and had him make me a magical new leg out of tin. The leg worked very well, once I was used to it. But my action angered the Wicked Witch of the East, for she had promised the old woman I should not marry the handsome Munchkin boy. When I began grinding again—Goblin scouts mostly, some warriors—my axe slipped and cut off my right leg. Again I went to the tinsmith, and again he made me a leg out of tin. After this the enchanted axe cut off my arms, one after the other; but, nothing daunted, I had them replaced with tin ones.

41

The Wicked Witch then made the axe slip and cut off my head, and at first I thought that was the end of me. But the Tinkerer had developed a strong curiosity about me—not to say friendship—and had a priest play *Raise Dead* after having made me a new head out of tin.

"I thought I had beaten the Wicked Witch then, and with a natural armor class of eighteen was levelling fast against her minions; I was just four kills away from level five; but I little knew how cruel my enemy could be. She thought of a new way to kill my love for the beautiful Munchkin youth, and made my axe slip again, so that it cut right through my body, splitting me into two halves. Once more the Tinkerer came to my help and made me a body of tin, fastening my tin arms and legs and head to it, by means of joints, so that I could move around as well as ever. But, alas! After my second *Raise Dead*, I found I had lost all my love for the Munchkin boy, and did not care to marry him. The moment I told him so, I was met with a divine message from the Goddess of Light that I had broken my Code of Conduct as a Paladin. My class features were all stripped away from me and I could no longer advance as a Paladin.

"I therefore decided to progress as an ordinary Warrior. And since my body had a natural armor class of twenty-five, I felt very proud of it and it did not matter now if my axe slipped, for it could not cut me. There was only one danger—that my joints would rust; but I kept an oil-can in my cottage and took care to oil myself whenever I needed it. However, there came a day when I forgot to do this, and, being caught in a rainstorm, before I thought of the danger my joints had rusted, and I was left to stand in the woods until you came to help me. It was a terrible thing to undergo, but during the year I stood there I had time to think that the greatest loss I had known was the loss of my Paladin class. While I was leveling fast as a Paladin, I was the happiest woman on earth; but no one can stay a Paladin who has broken the Code of Conduct, and so I am resolved to ask Oz to arrange an *Atonement*. If he does, I will go back to the Munchkin youth and marry him."

Both Dorothy and the Scarecrow had been greatly interested in the story of the Tin Woman, and now they knew why she was so anxious to get an *Atonement*. But she had not addressed the question of Intelligence versus Constitution.

"Why, isn't that obvious?" replied the Tin Warrior when asked to do so by Scarecrow (who had been worried his poor Intelligence had meant he had missed the point). "Paladins are divine casters. We need Wisdom not Intelligence for our spells. But above all, we are front line tanks and if I combine my unusually powerful natural armor with a big enough pool of hit points, we have an exploit that will allow my party to take out the most challenging of bosses."

"All the same," said the Scarecrow, "I shall ask for Intelligence instead of Constitution; for a Bard with a zero Intelligence is no use to anyone, most of all, himself."

"If I can have both *Atonement* and a stat increase, I shall take Constitution," returned the Tin Woman; "for tanking is the best thing in the world."

Dorothy did not say anything, for it seemed clear enough that your class determined your preferred attribute. She decided if she could only get back to Kansas and Aunt Em, it did not matter so much whether the Scarecrow had no Intelligence and the Tin Woman no progression as a Paladin, or each got what he or she wanted.

What worried her most was that the bread was nearly gone, and another meal for herself and Toto would empty the basket. To be sure, neither the Tin Woman nor the Scarecrow ever ate anything, but she did not have the *Endure without Sustenance* condition, and could not live unless she was fed.

CHAPTER VI

The Cowardly Lioness

All this time Dorothy and her companions had been walking through the thick woods. The road was still paved with yellow brick, but these were much covered by dried branches and dead leaves from the trees, and the walking was not at all good.

There were few birds in this part of the forest, for birds love the open country where there is plenty of sunshine. But now and then there came a deep growl from some wild animal hidden among the trees. These sounds made the little girl's heart beat fast, for she did not know what made them; but Toto knew, and he walked close to Dorothy's side, and did not even bark in return.

"How long will it be," the child asked of the Tin Woman, "before we are out of the forest?"

"I cannot tell," was the answer, "for I have never been to the Emerald City. But my father went there once, when I was a girl, and he said it was a long journey through a dangerous country, although nearer to the city where Oz dwells the country is beautiful. But I am not afraid so long as I have my oil-can, and nothing can hurt the Scarecrow. While you bear upon your forehead the *Protection from Evil* of the Good Witch's kiss, that will give you at least plus two on saves as well as immunity from the physical attacks of summoned evil creatures."

"But Toto!" said the girl anxiously. "What will protect him?"

"We must protect him ourselves if he is in danger," replied the Tin Woman.

Just as she spoke there came from the forest a terrible roar, and the next moment a great Lioness bounded into the road. With one blow of her paw she sent the Scarecrow spinning over and over to the edge of the road, and then she struck at the Tin Woman with her sharp claws. But, to the Lioness's surprise, she could make no impression on the tin, although the Tin Woman fell over in the road and lay still.

Little Toto, now that he had an enemy to face, ran barking toward the Lioness, and the great beast had opened her mouth to bite the dog, when Dorothy, fearing Toto would be killed in one hit, and heedless of drawing aggro, cast *Magic Missile* and threw it directly into the Lioness's nose, while crying out:

"Don't you dare to bite Toto! You ought to be ashamed of yourself, a big beast like you, to bite a poor little dog!"

"I didn't bite him," said the Lioness, as she rubbed her nose with her paw where Dorothy had hit it for an impressive 25 damage.

"No, but you tried to," Dorothy retorted. "You are nothing but a big coward."

"I know it," said the Lioness, hanging her head in shame. "I've always known it. But how can I help it?"

46

"I don't know, I'm sure. To think of your striking a stuffed man, like the poor Scarecrow!"

"Is he stuffed?" asked the Lioness in surprise, as she watched Dorothy pick up the Scarecrow and set him upon his feet, while she patted him into shape again.

"Of course he's stuffed," replied Dorothy, who was still angry.

"That's why he went over so easily," remarked the Lioness. "It astonished me to see him whirl around so. Is the other one stuffed also?"

"No," said Dorothy, "she's made of tin." And she helped the Tin Woman up again.

"That's why she nearly blunted my claws," said the Lioness. "When they scratched against the tin it made a cold shiver run down my back. I think it grants her a *Damage Shield* of at least twenty against sharp weapons.

"What is that little animal you are so tender of?"

"He is my familiar, Toto," answered Dorothy.

"Is he made of tin, or stuffed?" asked the Lioness.

"Neither. He's a—a—a meat dog," said the girl.

"Oh! He's a curious animal and seems remarkably small, now that I look at him. No one would think of biting such a little thing, except a coward like me," continued the Lioness sadly.

"What makes you a coward?" asked Dorothy, looking at the great beast in wonder, for she was as big as a small horse.

"It's a *Curse* from the Wicked Witch of the East," replied the Lioness. "I am a level seven Barbarian and ought to be able to

Rage. All the other animals in the forest naturally expect me to Rage, for the Lioness is everywhere thought to be the Queen of Beasts. But I've been stripped of that ability. Instead, I learned that if I roared very loudly every living thing was frightened and got out of my way. Whenever I've met a man I've been awfully scared; but I just roared at him, and he has always run away as fast as he could go. If the elephants and the tigers and the bears had ever tried to fight me, I should have run myself—I'm such a coward without Rage; but just as soon as they hear me roar they all try to get away from me, and of course I let them go."

"But that isn't right. The Queen of Beasts shouldn't be a coward," said the Scarecrow.

"I know it," returned the Lioness, wiping a tear from her eye with the tip of her tail. "It is my great sorrow, and makes my life very unhappy. But whenever there is danger and I cannot Rage in order to face it, my heart begins to beat fast."

"But you can still level up in Barbarian?" asked the Tin Woman.

"It may be," said the Lioness. "I cannot tell, since I dare not fight meaningful opponents anymore."

"If you can," continued the Tin Woman, "you ought to be glad, for there is nothing better than levelling. For my part, I cannot continue with my Paladin class; and as a simple Warrior I'm only level two."

"Perhaps," said the Lioness thoughtfully, "if I could regain my Rage powers, I could finally reach level eight."

"Have you much Intelligence?" asked the Scarecrow.

"I suppose nine is quite good for a Barbarian," replied the Lioness.

"I am going to the Great Oz to ask him to give me some," remarked the Scarecrow, "for my head is stuffed with straw after the same Witch *Cursed* me and *Polymorphed* me."

"And I am going to ask him to *Atone* me," said the Tin Woman.

"And I am going to ask him to *Teleport* Toto and me back to Kansas," added Dorothy.

"Do you think Oz could give me back my Rage powers?" asked the Cowardly Barbarian Lioness.

"Just as easily as he could give me Intelligence," said the Scarecrow Bard.

"Or give me back my class," said the Tin Warrior.

"Or TP me back to Kansas," said Dorothy the Sorceress.

"Then, if you don't mind, I'll go with you," said the Lioness, "for my life is simply unbearable without being able to Rage."

"You will be very welcome," answered Dorothy, "for you will help to keep away the other wild beasts. It seems to me they must be more cowardly than you are if they allow you to scare them so easily."

"They really are," said the Lioness, "but that doesn't make me any braver, and as long as I know myself to be unable to Rage I shall be unhappy."

So once more Dorothy issued a group invite and the little company set off upon the journey, the Lioness walking with stately strides at Dorothy's side. Toto did not approve of this new comrade at first, for he could not forget how nearly he had been crushed between the Lioness's great jaws. But after a time he became more at ease, and presently Toto and the Cowardly Lioness had grown to be good friends.

During the rest of that day there was no other adventure, which was slightly disappointing to Dorothy, who now she had a tank in the party was keen to test the effect of *Haste*. She looked hopefully at every distant rustle in the undergrowth of the forest, but there came no opportunity for a battle.

Once, indeed, the Tin Woman stepped upon a beetle that was crawling along the road, and killed the poor little thing. This made the Tin Woman very unhappy, for she was always careful not to hurt any living creature unless it gave her XP or loot; and as she walked along she wept several tears of sorrow and regret. These tears ran slowly down her face and over the hinges of her jaw, and there they rusted. When Dorothy presently asked her a question the Tin Woman could not open her mouth, for her jaws were tightly rusted together. She became greatly frightened at this and made many motions to Dorothy to relieve her, but Dorothy could not understand. The Lioness was also puzzled to know what was wrong. But the Scarecrow seized the oil-can from Dorothy's basket and oiled the Tin Woman's jaws, so that after a few moments she could talk as well as before.

"This will serve me a lesson," said she, "to look where I step. For if I should kill another bug or beetle I should surely cry again, and crying rusts my jaws so that I cannot speak."

Thereafter she walked very carefully, with her eyes on the road, and when she saw a tiny ant toiling by she would step over it, so as not to harm it. The Tin Woman knew very well she had lost her Paladin status, and therefore she took great care never to be cruel or unkind to anything.

"You people," she said, "have your good alignments"—Scarecrow and Dorothy exchanged an uneasy glance—"to guide you, and need never worry unduly about your actions: you just need to be yourself; but ever since losing my Paladin class, I no longer have the Code of Conduct to guide me, and so I must be extra careful to be good. When Oz gives that to me, of course, I needn't mind so much and could probably come up with justifications for killing any mob, especially if there was experience or loot to gain."

Smiling approvingly, Scarecrow linked arms and the four newly found friends skipped along merrily, singing songs about levelling up, loot and magic items.

CHAPTER VII

The Journey to the Great Oz

The party was obliged to camp out that night under a large tree in the forest, for there were no houses near. The tree made a good, thick covering to protect them from the dew, and the Tin Woman chopped a great pile of wood with her axe and Dorothy built a splendid fire that warmed her and made her feel less lonely. She and Toto ate the last of their bread, and now she did not know what they would do for breakfast.

"If you wish," said the Lioness, "I will go into the forest and kill a deer for you. You can roast it by the fire, since your tastes are so peculiar that you prefer cooked food, and then you will have a very good breakfast."

"Don't! Please don't," begged the Tin Woman. "I should certainly weep if you killed a poor deer without sharing the XP from the kill, and then my jaws would rust again."

But the Lioness went away into the forest and found her own supper, and no one ever knew what it was, for she didn't mention it. And the Scarecrow found a tree full of nuts and filled Dorothy's basket with them, so that she would not be hungry for a long time. She thought this was very kind and thoughtful of the Scarecrow, but she laughed heartily at the awkward way in which the poor creature picked up the nuts. His padded hands were so clumsy and the nuts were so small that he dropped almost as many as he put in the basket. But the Scarecrow did not mind how long it took him to fill the basket, for it enabled him to keep away from the fire, as he feared a spark might get into his straw and burn him up. So he kept a good distance away from the flames, and only came near to cover Dorothy with dry leaves when she lay down to sleep. These kept her very snug and warm, and she slept soundly until morning.

When it was daylight, the girl bathed her face in a little rippling brook, and soon after they all started toward the Emerald City.

This was to be an eventful day for the travelers. They had hardly been walking an hour when they saw before them a great ditch that crossed the road and divided the forest as far as they could see on either side. It was a very wide ditch, and when they crept up to the edge and looked into it they could see it was also very deep, and there were many big, jagged rocks at the bottom. The sides were so steep that none of them could climb down, and for a moment it seemed that their journey must end.

"What shall we do?" asked Dorothy despairingly.

"I haven't the faintest idea," said the Tin Woman, and the Lioness shook her long face and looked thoughtful.

But the Scarecrow said, "We cannot fly, that is certain until Dorothy can scribe the *Fly* spell into her spellbook. Neither can we climb down into this great ditch. Therefore, if we cannot jump over it, we must stop where we are."

"I think I could jump over it," said the Cowardly Lioness, after measuring the distance carefully in her mind. "My Acrobatics is eighteen and it doesn't matter that I cannot Rage."

"Then we are all right," answered the Scarecrow, "for you can carry us all over on your back, one at a time."

"I can cast *Haste*," offered Dorothy, "it doesn't improve Acrobatics but perhaps base movement comes into play here too, in which case it will help a lot."

"Well, I'll try it," said the Lioness. "Who will go first?"

"I will," declared the Scarecrow, "for, if you found that you could not jump over the gulf, Dorothy would be killed, or the Tin Woman badly dented on the rocks below. But if I am on your back it will not matter so much, for the fall would not hurt me at all."

"I am terribly afraid of falling, myself," said the Cowardly Lioness, "but I suppose there is nothing to do but try it. So get on my back and we will make the attempt."

The Scarecrow sat upon the Lioness's back, and after Dorothy had cast *Haste* the big beast walked to the edge of the gulf and crouched down.

"Why don't you run and jump?" asked the Scarecrow.

"Because that isn't the way we Lionesses do these things," she replied. Then giving a great spring, she shot through the air and landed safely on the other side. They were all greatly pleased to see how easily she did it, and after the Scarecrow had got down from her back the Lioness sprang across the ditch again.

Dorothy thought she would go next; so she took Toto in her arms and climbed on the Lioness's back, holding tightly to her soft ruff with one hand. The next moment it seemed as if she were flying through the air; and then, before she had time to think about it, she was safe on the other side. The Lioness went back a third time and got the Tin Woman, and then they all sat down for a few moments to give the beast a chance to rest, for her great leaps had made her breath short, and she panted like a big dog that had been running too long.

They found the forest very thick on this side, and it looked dark and gloomy. After the Lioness had rested they started along the road of yellow brick, silently wondering, each in his or her own mind, if ever they would come to the end of the woods and reach the bright sunshine again. To add to their discomfort, they soon heard strange noises in the depths of the forest, and the Lioness whispered to them that it was in this part of the country that the Kalidahs lived.

"What are the Kalidahs?" asked the girl.

"They are monstrous beasts with bodies like bears and heads like tigers," replied the Lioness, "and with claws so long and sharp that they could tear me in two as easily as I could kill Toto. I'm terribly afraid of the Kalidahs."

"I'm not surprised that you are," returned Dorothy. "They must be dreadful beasts. What level are they?"

The Lioness was about to reply when suddenly they came to another gulf across the road. But this one was so broad and deep that the Lioness knew at once she could not leap across it.

So they sat down to consider what they should do, and after serious thought the Scarecrow said:

"Here is a great tree, standing close to the ditch. If the Tin Woman can chop it down, so that it will fall to the other side, we can walk across it easily."

"That is a first-rate idea," said the Lioness. "One would almost suspect you had Intelligence in your head, despite the straw."

The Tin Woman set to work at once, and so sharp was her axe that the tree was soon chopped nearly through. Then the Lioness put her strong front legs against the tree and pushed with all her might, and slowly the big tree tipped and fell with a crash across the ditch, with its top branches on the other side.

They had just started to cross this queer bridge when a sharp growl made them all look up, and to their horror they saw running toward them two great beasts with bodies like bears and heads like tigers.

"They are the Kalidahs!" said the Cowardly Lioness, beginning to tremble.

"Quick!" cried the Scarecrow. "Let us cross over."

Dorothy attempted a Knowledge Nature check but only discovered that the approaching enemies were both level ten. That was enough to know that to hope for victory was impossible, especially as they had no healer. Even the Tin Woman wouldn't be able to tank them for long.

Instead of wasting time in casting a spell, Dorothy ran onto the tree, holding Toto in her arms, the Tin Woman followed, and the Scarecrow came next. The Lioness, although she was certainly afraid, turned to face the Kalidahs, and then she gave so loud and terrible a roar that Dorothy screamed and the Scarecrow fell over backward, while even the fierce beasts stopped short and looked at her in surprise.

But, seeing they were three levels higher than the Lioness, and remembering that there were two of them and only one of her, the Kalidahs again rushed forward, and the Lioness crossed over the tree and turned to see what they would do next. Without stopping an instant the fierce beasts also began to cross the tree.

Dorothy began to cast and the Lioness turned to her and said:

"We are lost, for they will surely tear us to pieces with their sharp claws. But I will fight them as long as I am alive and perhaps give you time to complete that spell."

"Wait a minute!" called the Scarecrow. He had been thinking what was best to be done, "we need to push our end of the tree into the chasm."

But even with the Tin Woman, the Scarecrow and the Lioness pushing as hard as they could while Dorothy chanted, the tree was stuck.

"If only I could Rage," groaned the Lioness.

"If only I could sing an inspiring song," mourned the Scarecrow.

"If only I could cast *Protection from Evil*," cried the Tin Woman.

Just as the two Kalidahs were nearly across, the spell that Dorothy had been casting completed at last. It was a *Stinking Cloud*, placed on the monsters and covering the remainder of their path across the tree trunk. Retching and coughing, the Kalidahs had clearly failed their resistance checks and falling down Nauseated, rolled off the narrow tree trunk. Both were dashed to pieces on the sharp rocks at the bottom.

You have killed two Kalidahs.
XP +12,000

"Well done, Dorothy," said the Cowardly Lioness, drawing a long breath of relief, "I see we are going to live a little while longer, and I am glad of it, for it must be a very uncomfortable thing not to be alive. Those creatures frightened me so badly that my heart is beating yet, despite the impressive XP gain."

"Ah," said the Tin Woman sadly, "I wish I had a Paladin Class to put those XP points into. Still, I can't complain for I am nearly level three in Warrior."

"I wonder did they have loot on them?" Scarecrow peered over the lip of the chasm's edge and although he thought that it would be easy for him to drop down to loot the dead, he also thought that it would be impossible for him to get up again.

This adventure made the travelers more anxious than ever to get out of the forest; the wandering monsters were just too high level. The party members walked so fast that Dorothy became tired, and had to ride on the Lioness's back. This proved to be a smart solution to speeding up their rate of travel, for Dorothy could cast *Haste* twice, depleting her mana for sixteen minutes of improved mobility. Then she could sit on the Lioness while her mana replenished.

To their great joy the trees became thinner the farther they advanced, and in the afternoon they suddenly came upon a broad river, flowing swiftly just before them. On the other side of the water they could see the road of yellow brick running through a beautiful country, with green meadows dotted with bright flowers and all the road bordered with trees hanging full of delicious fruits. They were greatly pleased to see this delightful country before them.

"How shall we cross the river?" asked Dorothy.

"That is easily done," replied the Scarecrow. "The Tin Woman must build us a raft, so we can float to the other side."

So the Tin Woman took her axe and began to chop down small trees to make a raft, and while she was busy at this the Scarecrow found on the riverbank a tree full of fine fruit. This pleased Dorothy, who had eaten nothing but nuts all day, and she made a hearty meal of the ripe fruit.

But it takes time to make a raft, even when one has the Craft Wooden Item skill capped at 35, as the Tin Woman did, and when night came the work was not done. So they found a cozy place under the trees where they slept well until the morning; and Dorothy dreamed of the Emerald City, and of the good Wizard Oz, who would soon *Teleport* her back to her own home again.

CHAPTER VIII

The Deadly Poppy Field

Our little party of travelers awakened the next morning refreshed and full of hope, and Dorothy breakfasted like a princess off peaches and plums from the trees beside the river. Behind them was the dark forest they had passed safely through, although they had suffered many discouragements; but before them was a lovely, sunny country that seemed to beckon them on to the Emerald City.

To be sure, the broad river now cut them off from this beautiful land. But the raft was nearly done, and after the Tin Woman had cut a few more logs and fastened them together with wooden pins, they were ready to start. Dorothy sat down in the middle of the raft and held Toto in her arms. When the Cowardly Lioness stepped upon the raft it tipped badly, for she was big and heavy and the Tin Woman had only just made her crafting check; but the Scarecrow and the Tin Woman stood upon the other end to steady it, and they had long poles in their hands to push the raft through the water.

They got along quite well at first, but when they reached the middle of the river the swift current swept the raft downstream, farther and farther away from the road of yellow brick. And the water grew so deep that the long poles would not touch the bottom.

"This is bad," said the Tin Woman, "for if we cannot get to the land we shall be carried into the country of the Wicked Witch of the West, and she will enchant us and make us her slaves."

"And then I should get no Intelligence restored," said the Scarecrow.

"And I should get no Rage," said the Cowardly Lioness.

"And I should get no Paladin Class," said the Tin Woman.

"And I should never get back to Kansas," said Dorothy.

"We must certainly get to the Emerald City if we can," the Scarecrow continued, and he pushed so hard on his long pole that it stuck fast in the mud at the bottom of the river. Then, before he could pull it out again—or let go—the raft was swept away, and the poor Scarecrow was left clinging to the pole in the middle of the river.

"Good-bye!" he called after them, and they were very sorry to leave him. Indeed, the Tin Woman began to cry, but fortunately remembered that she might rust, and so dried her tears on Dorothy's apron.

Of course this was a bad thing for the Scarecrow.

"I am now worse off than when I first met Dorothy," he thought. "Then, I was tied a pole in a cornfield, I could try to earn XP by completing the task of scaring away giant rats and crows, at any rate. But surely there is no use for a Scarecrow Bard without spells or abilities, stuck on a pole in the middle of a river. I am afraid I shall never have any Intelligence again, after all!"

Down the stream the raft floated, and the poor Scarecrow was left far behind. Then the Lioness said:

"Something must be done to save us. Although my Swim skill is only seven, I think I should try to swim to the shore and pull the raft after me, if you will only hold fast to the tip of my tail."

So she sprang into the water, and the Tin Woman caught fast hold of her tail. Then the Lioness began to swim with all her might toward the shore. It was hard work: she was so big and her checks were a mix of success and failure; but there were no fumbles, so by and by they were drawn out of the current, and then Dorothy took the Tin Woman's long pole and helped push the raft to the land.

They were all tired out when they reached the shore at last and stepped off upon the pretty green grass, and they also knew that the stream had carried them a long way past the road of yellow brick that led to the Emerald City.

"What shall we do now?" asked the Tin Woman, as the Lioness lay down on the grass to let the sun dry her.

"We must get back to the road, in some way," said Dorothy.

"And to our friend, the Scarecrow," added the Tin Woman. "A Paladin… that is to say, a Warrior never abandons a companion."

"The best plan will be to walk along the riverbank until we come to Scarecrow again and after that, the road," remarked the Lioness.

So, when they were rested, Dorothy picked up her basket and they started along the grassy bank, to the road from which the river had carried them. It was a lovely country, with plenty of flowers and fruit trees and sunshine to cheer them, and had they not felt so sorry for the poor Scarecrow, they could have been very happy.

They walked along as fast as they could, Dorothy only stopping once to pick a beautiful flower; and after a time the Tin Woman cried out: "Look!"

Then they all looked at the river and saw the Scarecrow perched upon his pole in the middle of the water, looking very lonely and sad.

"What can we do to save him?" asked Dorothy.

The Lioness and the Tin Woman both shook their heads, for they did not know. So they sat down upon the bank and gazed wistfully at the Scarecrow until a Stork flew by, who, upon seeing them, stopped to rest at the water's edge.

"Who are you and where are you going?" asked the Stork.

"I am Dorothy," answered the girl, "and these are my friends, the Tin Woman and the Cowardly Lioness; and we are going to the Emerald City."

"This isn't the road," said the Stork, as she twisted her long neck and looked sharply at the queer party.

"I know it," returned Dorothy, "but we have lost the Scarecrow, and are wondering how we shall get him again."

"Where is he?" asked the Stork.

"Over there in the river," answered the little girl.

"If he wasn't so big and heavy I would get him for you," remarked the Stork.

"He isn't heavy a bit," said Dorothy eagerly, "for he is stuffed with straw; and if you will bring him back to us, we shall thank you ever and ever so much."

"Well, I'll try," said the Stork, "but if I find he is too heavy to carry I shall have to drop him in the river again."

So the big bird flew into the air and over the water till she came to where the Scarecrow was perched upon his pole. Then the Stork with her great claws grabbed the Scarecrow by the arm and carried him up into the air and back to the bank, where Dorothy and the Lioness and the Tin Woman and Toto were sitting.

When the Scarecrow found himself among his friends again, he was so happy that he hugged them all, even the Lioness and Toto; and as they walked along he sang "Tol-de-ri-de-oh!" at every step, he felt so cheerful.

"I was afraid I should have to stay in the river forever," he said, "but the kind Stork saved me and if I ever get my Intelligence back, and with it my Bard spells and abilities, I shall find the Stork again and do her some kindness in return."

"That's all right," said the Stork, who was flying along beside them. "I always like to help anyone in trouble. But I must go now, for my babies are waiting in the nest for me. I hope you will find the Emerald City and that Oz will help you."

"Thank you," replied Dorothy, and then the kind Stork flew into the air and was soon out of sight.

They walked along listening to the singing of the brightly colored birds and looking at the lovely flowers which now became so thick that the ground was carpeted with them. There were big yellow and white and blue and purple blossoms, besides great clusters of scarlet poppies, which were so brilliant in color they almost dazzled Dorothy's eyes.

"Aren't they beautiful?" the girl asked, as she breathed in the spicy scent of the bright flowers.

"I suppose so," answered the Scarecrow. "When I have Intelligence, I shall probably like them better."

"If I only had an *Atonement*, I should recover my feelings of love," added the Tin Woman. "Then I would present these flowers to the boy of my heart."

"I always did like flowers," said the Lioness. "They seem so helpless and frail. But there are none in the forest so bright as these."

They now came upon more and more of the big scarlet poppies, and fewer and fewer of the other flowers; and soon they found themselves in the midst of a great meadow of *Poppies of Slumber*. Now it is well known that when there are many of these flowers together their odor is so powerful that anyone who breathes it and fails their will save falls asleep, and if the sleeper is not carried away from the scent of the flowers, she sleeps on and on forever. But Dorothy did not know this, nor could she get away from the bright red flowers that were everywhere about; so when eventually she failed her will check, as was inevitable, her eyes grew heavy and she felt she must sit down to rest and to sleep.

But the Tin Woman would not let her do this.

"We must hurry and get back to the road of yellow brick before dark," she said; and the Scarecrow agreed with her.

Although only half awake, Dorothy could see the value of casting *Haste* on the entire party. That helped and they kept walking at the additional speed until after two uses of the spell Dorothy's mana pool was exhausted and soon after, she found she could stand no longer. Her eyes closed in spite of herself and she forgot where she was and fell among the poppies, fast asleep.

"What shall we do?" asked the Tin Woman.

"If we leave her here she will die," said the Lioness. "The smell of the flowers is killing us all. I myself can scarcely keep my eyes open, and the dog is asleep already."

It was true; Toto had finally failed his will save, despite a +6 Magic Resistance, and fallen down beside his little mistress. But the Scarecrow and the Tin Woman, both having the *No Breath* buff as a condition, were not troubled by the scent of the flowers.

"Run fast," said the Scarecrow to the Lioness, "and get out of this deadly flower bed as soon as you can. We will bring the little girl with us, but if you should fall asleep you are too big to be carried."

So the Lioness aroused herself and bounded forward as fast as she could go. In a moment she was out of sight.

"Let us make a chair with our hands and carry her," said the Scarecrow. So they picked up Toto and put the dog in Dorothy's lap, and then they made a chair with their hands for the seat and their arms for the arms and carried the sleeping girl between them through the flowers.

On and on they walked, and it seemed that the great carpet of deadly flowers that surrounded them would never end. They followed the bend of the river, and at last came upon their friend the Lioness, lying fast asleep among the poppies. The flowers had been too strong for the huge beast and she had failed her resistance check only a short distance from the end of the poppy bed, where the sweet grass spread in beautiful green fields before them.

"We can do nothing for her," said the Tin Woman sadly; "for she is much too heavy to lift. We must leave her here to sleep on forever, and perhaps she will dream that she has restored her Rage at last."

"I'm sorry," said the Scarecrow. "The Lioness was a very good comrade for one so afflicted. If only she had Rage, she would have been immune to the effect of the poppies. But let us go on."

They carried the sleeping girl to a pretty spot beside the river, far enough from the poppy field to prevent her breathing any more of the poison of the flowers, and here they laid her gently on the soft grass and waited for the fresh breeze to waken her.

CHAPTER IX

The Queen of the Field Mice

"We cannot be far from the road of yellow brick, now," remarked the Scarecrow, as he stood beside the girl, "for we have come nearly as far as the river carried us away."

The Tin Woman was about to reply when she heard a low growl, and turning her head (which worked beautifully on hinges) she saw a strange beast come bounding over the grass toward them. It was, indeed, a great yellow Wildcat, and the Tin Woman thought it must be chasing something, for its ears were lying close to its head and its mouth was wide open, showing two rows of ugly teeth, while its red eyes glowed like balls of fire. As it came nearer the Tin Woman saw that running before the beast was a little gray field mouse, and although she no longer had the Paladin Code of Conduct to guide her, she knew it was wrong for the Wildcat to try to kill such a pretty, harmless creature. Especially because by being in the wrong, the Wildcat could be killed and its XP gained legitimately.

So the Tin Woman raised her axe, and as the Wildcat ran by she gave it a quick blow that was a critical hit! She saw the following message flash by:

```
Critical hit!
You have struck a Wildcat for 76 damage!


You have killed a Wildcat.
XP +350
```

The former Paladin had cut the beast's head clean off from its body, and the creature rolled over at her feet in two pieces.

The field mouse, now that it was freed from its enemy, stopped short; and coming slowly up to the Tin Woman it said, in a squeaky little voice:

"Oh, thank you! Thank you ever so much for saving my life."

"Don't speak of it, I beg of you," replied the Tin Woman. "I no longer have the Paladin Code of Conduct to live by, you know, so I am careful to help all those who may need a friend, even if it happens to be only a mouse."

"Only a mouse!" cried the little animal, indignantly. "Why, I am a Queen—the Queen of all the Field Mice!"

"Oh, indeed," said the Tin Woman, making a bow.

"Therefore you have done a great deed, as well as a brave one, in saving my life," added the Queen.

At that moment several mice were seen running up as fast as their little legs could carry them, and when they saw their Queen they exclaimed:

"Oh, your Majesty, we thought you would be killed! How did you manage to escape the great Wildcat?" They all bowed so low to the little Queen that they almost stood upon their heads.

"This funny metal woman," she answered, "killed the Wildcat and saved my life. So hereafter you must all serve her, and obey her slightest wish."

"We will!" cried all the mice, in a shrill chorus. And then they scampered in all directions, for Toto had awakened from his sleep, and seeing all these mice around him he gave one bark of delight and jumped right into the middle of the group. Toto had always loved to chase mice when he lived in Kansas, and he saw no harm in it.

But the Tin Woman caught the dog in her arms and held him tight, while she called to the mice, "Come back! Come back! Toto shall not hurt you."

At this the Queen of the Mice stuck her head out from underneath a clump of grass and asked, in a timid voice, "Are you sure he will not bite us?"

"I will not let him," said the Tin Woman; "so do not be afraid."

One by one the mice came creeping back, and Toto did not bark again, although he tried to get out of the Tin Woman's arms, and would have bitten her had he not known very well she was made of tin. Finally one of the biggest mice spoke.

"Is there anything we can do," it asked, "to repay you for saving the life of our Queen?"

71

"Nothing that I know of," answered the Tin Woman; but the Scarecrow, who had been trying to think, but could not because his Intelligence was 0, said, quickly, "Oh, yes; you can save our friend, the Cowardly Lioness, who is asleep in the poppy bed."

"A Lioness!" cried the little Queen. "Why, she would eat us all up."

"Oh, no," declared the Scarecrow; "this Lioness is a coward."

"Really?" asked the Mouse.

"She says so herself," answered the Scarecrow, "and she would never hurt anyone who is our friend. If you will help us to save her I promise that she shall treat you all with kindness."

"Very well," said the Queen, "we trust you. But what shall we do?"

"Are there many of these mice which call you Queen and are willing to obey you?"

"Oh, yes; there are thousands," she replied.

"Then send for them all to come here as soon as possible, and let each one bring a long piece of string."

The Queen turned to the mice that attended her and told them to go at once and get all her people. As soon as they heard her orders they ran away in every direction as fast as possible.

"Now," said the Scarecrow to the Tin Woman, "you must go to those trees by the riverside and make a cart that will carry the Lioness."

So the Tin Woman went at once to the trees and began to work. Her Craft Wooden Item skill was maxed at 35 and she soon made a low cart out of the limbs of trees, from which she chopped away all the leaves and branches. She fastened it together with wooden pegs and made the four wheels out of short pieces of a big tree trunk. So fast and so well did she work that by the time the mice began to arrive the cart was all ready for them.

They came from all directions, and there were thousands of them: big mice and little mice and middle-sized mice; and each one brought a piece of string in its mouth. It was about this time that Dorothy woke from her long sleep and opened her eyes. She was greatly astonished to find herself lying upon the grass, with thousands of mice standing around and looking at her timidly. But the Scarecrow told her about everything, and turning to the dignified little Mouse, he said:

"Permit me to introduce to you her Majesty, the Queen."

Dorothy nodded gravely and the Queen made a curtsy, after which she became quite friendly with the little girl.

The Scarecrow and the Tin Woman now began to fasten the mice to the truck, using the strings they had brought. One end of a string was tied around the neck of each mouse and the other end to the cart. Of course the cart was a thousand times bigger than any of the mice who were to draw it; but when all the mice had been harnessed, they were able to pull it quite easily. Even the Scarecrow and the Tin Woman could sit on it, and were drawn swiftly by their queer little horses to the place where the Lioness lay asleep.

After a great deal of hard work, for the Lioness was heavy, they managed to get her up on the truck. Then the Queen hurriedly gave her people the order to start, for she feared if the mice stayed among the poppies too long they also would fall asleep.

At first the little creatures, many though they were, could hardly stir the heavily loaded truck; but the Tin Woman and the Scarecrow both pushed from behind, and they got along better. Soon they rolled the Lioness out of the poppy bed to the green fields, where she could breathe the sweet, fresh air again, instead of the poisonous scent of the flowers.

Dorothy came to meet them and thanked the little mice warmly for saving her companion from death. She had grown so fond of the big Lioness she was glad she had been rescued.

Then the mice were unharnessed from the truck and scampered away through the grass to their homes. The Queen of the Mice was the last to leave.

"If ever you need us again," she said, "come out into the field and call, and we shall hear you and come to your assistance. Good-bye!"

"Good-bye!" they all answered, and away the Queen ran, while Dorothy held Toto tightly lest he should run after her and frighten her.

After this they sat down beside the Lioness until she should awaken; and the Scarecrow brought Dorothy some fruit from a tree nearby, which she ate for her dinner.

CHAPTER X

The Guardian of the Gate

It was some time before the Cowardly Lioness awakened, for she had lain among the poppies a long while, breathing in their deadly fragrance; but when she did open her eyes and roll off the truck she was very glad to find herself still alive.

"I ran as fast as I could," she said, sitting down and yawning, "but the flowers were too strong for me. How did you get me out?"

Then they told her of the field mice, and how they had generously saved her from death; and the Cowardly Lioness laughed, and said:

"I have always thought myself very big and terrible; yet such little things as flowers came near to killing me, and such small animals as mice have saved my life. How strange it all is! But, comrades, what shall we do now?"

"We must journey on until we find the road of yellow brick again," said Dorothy, "and then we can keep on to the Emerald City."

So, the Lioness being fully refreshed, and feeling quite herself again, they all started upon the journey, greatly enjoying the walk through the soft, fresh grass; and it was not long before they reached the road of yellow brick and turned again toward the Emerald City where the Great Oz dwelt.

The road was smooth and well paved, now, and the country about was beautiful, so that the travelers rejoiced in leaving the forest far behind, and with it the many dangers they had met in its gloomy shades. Dorothy and Toto played hide and seek, using their *Hide* and *Perception* skills alternately, until they were maxed (at 40 for Dorothy and 25 for Toto).

Once more they could see fences built beside the road; but these were painted green, and when they came to a small house, in which an NPC farmer evidently lived, that also was painted green. They passed by several of these houses during the afternoon, and sometimes people came to the doors and looked at them as if they would like to ask questions; but no one came near them nor spoke to them because of the great Lioness, of which they were very much afraid. The people were all dressed in clothing of a lovely emerald-green color and wore peaked hats like those of the Munchkins.

"This must be the Land of Oz," said Dorothy, "and we are surely getting near the Emerald City."

"Yes," answered the Scarecrow. "Everything is green here, while in the country of the Munchkins blue was the favorite color. But the people do not seem to be as friendly as the Munchkins, and I'm afraid that without any of my Bard abilities being available we shall be unable to find a place to pass the night."

"I should like something to eat besides fruit," said the girl, "and I'm sure Toto is nearly starved. Let us stop at the next house and talk to the people."

So, when they came to a good-sized farmhouse, Dorothy walked boldly up to the door and knocked.

A woman opened it just far enough to look out, and said, "What do you want, child, and why is that great Lioness with you?"

"We wish to pass the night with you, if you will allow us," answered Dorothy; "and the Lioness is my friend and comrade, and would not hurt you for the world."

"Is she tame?" asked the woman, opening the door a little wider.

"Oh, yes," said the girl, attempting to use her *Persuasion* skill, although it was only 3 through lack of practice, "and she is a great coward, too. She will be more afraid of you than you are of her."

"Well, I don't know," said the woman, unimpressed by Dorothy. But she looked again at Lioness who pulled such a ferocious face that the NPC failed a check against being *Intimidated*. "If that is the case you may come in, and I will give you some supper and a place to sleep."

So they all entered the house, where there were, besides the woman, two children and a man. The man was lying on the couch in a corner. As was often the case with NPCs, they did not seem particularly surprised to see so strange a company, as if a party of adventurers coming inside was perfectly normal.

While the woman was busy laying the table, Scarecrow sighed.

"I wish I had my Bardic powers, for then I could make friends with these people and we could interrogate… I mean find out what they know about the Mighty Oz."

The man asked:

"You mention the fearsome Oz? Where are you going?"

"To the Emerald City," said Dorothy, "to see the Great Oz."

"Oh, indeed!" exclaimed the man. "Are you sure that Oz will see you?"

"Why not?" she replied.

"Why, it is said that he never lets anyone come into his presence. I have been to the Emerald City many times, and it is a beautiful and wonderful place; but I have never been permitted to see the Great Oz, nor do I know of any living person who has seen him."

"Does he never go out?" asked the Scarecrow.

"Never. He sits day after day in the great Throne Room of his Palace, and even those who wait upon him do not see him face to face."

"What is he like?" asked the girl.

"That is hard to tell," said the man thoughtfully. "You see, Oz is a Great Wizard with a ring of *Polymorph Self*, and can take on any form he wishes. So that some say he looks like a bird; and some say he looks like an elephant; and some say he looks like a cat. To others he appears as a beautiful fairy, or a brownie, or in any other form that pleases him. But who the real Oz is, when he is in his own form, no living person can tell."

"That is very strange," said Dorothy, "but we must try, in some way, to see him, or we shall have made our journey for nothing."

"Why do you wish to see the terrible Oz?" asked the man.

"I want him to restore my Intelligence from the effects of a *Curse*," said the Scarecrow eagerly.

"Oh, Oz could do that easily enough," declared the man. "He has the most powerful *Dispel Magic* in all the land."

"And I want him to give me an *Atonement*," said the Tin Woman. "So I can resume my class as a Paladin."

"That will not trouble him," continued the man, "for Oz has a large collection of scrolls he can cast, of all levels and types of magic."

"And I want him to give me Rage back," said the Cowardly Lioness.

"Oz keeps a great pot of *Restoration* potion in his Throne Room," said the man, "which he has covered with a golden plate, to keep it from running over. He will be glad to give you some."

"And I want him to send me back to Kansas," said Dorothy.

"Where is Kansas?" asked the man, with surprise.

"I don't know," replied Dorothy sorrowfully, "but it is my home, and I'm sure it's somewhere."

"Very likely. Well, Oz can do anything; so I suppose he will find Kansas for you. But first you must get to see him, and that will be a hard task; for the Great Wizard does not like to see anyone, and he usually has his own way. But what do YOU want?" he continued, speaking to Toto. Toto only wagged his tail; for, strange to say, he could not speak. He could, however, communicate with Dorothy, who smiled and spoke for him.

"Toto would like another level and for me to learn an *Enlarge* spell, so he can be as big and savage as the Lioness."

The woman now called to them that supper was ready, so they gathered around the table and Dorothy ate some delicious porridge and a dish of scrambled eggs and a plate of nice white bread, and enjoyed her meal. The Lioness ate some of the porridge, but did not care for it, saying it was made from oats and oats were food for horses, not for Lionesses. Having the *Unending Sustenance* condition Scarecrow and the Tin Woman ate nothing at all. Toto ate a little of everything, and was glad to get a good supper again.

The woman now gave Dorothy a bed to sleep in, and Toto lay down beside her, while the Lioness guarded the door of her room so she might not be attacked or robbed if the NPCs turned hostile. The Scarecrow and the Tin Woman stood up in a corner and kept quiet all night, although of course they could not sleep.

The next morning, as soon as the sun was up, they started on their way, and soon saw a beautiful green glow in the sky just before them.

"That must be the Emerald City," said Dorothy.

As they walked on, the green glow became brighter and brighter, and it seemed that at last they were nearing the end of their travels. Yet it was afternoon before they came to the great wall that surrounded the City. It was high and thick and of a bright green color.

In front of them, and at the end of the road of yellow brick, was a big gate, all studded with emeralds that glittered so much in the sun that even the painted eyes of the Scarecrow were dazzled by their brilliancy.

"I wonder if it's possible to loot those?" muttered Scarecrow.

"Even though I no longer adhere to the Code of Conduct for Paladins," answered the Tin Woman, "I know that would be wrong."

"Might they be evil gems?" offered the Lioness.

After a short pause, the Tin Woman shook her head. "I think not."

There was a bell beside the gate, and Dorothy pushed the button and heard a silvery tinkle sound within. Then the big gate swung slowly open, and they all passed through and found themselves in a high arched room, the walls of which glistened with countless emeralds.

Before them stood a little man about the same size as the Munchkins. He was clothed all in green, from his head to his feet, and even his skin was of a greenish tint. At his side was a large green box.

When he saw Dorothy and her companions the man asked, "What do you wish in the Emerald City?"

"We came here to see the Great Oz," said Dorothy.

The man was so surprised at this answer that he sat down to think it over.

"It has been many years since anyone asked me to see Oz," he said, shaking his head in perplexity. "He is powerful and terrible, and if you come on an idle or foolish errand to bother the wise reflections of the Great Wizard, he might be angry and destroy you all in an instant."

"But it is not a foolish errand, nor an idle one," replied the Scarecrow; "it is important. And we have been told that Oz is a Lawful Good Wizard."

"So he is," said the green man, "and he rules the Emerald City wisely and well. But to those who are not honest, or who approach him from curiosity, he is most terrible, and few have ever dared ask to see his face. I am the Guardian of the Gates, and since you demand to see the Great Oz I must take you to his Palace. But first you must put on the spectacles."

"Why?" asked Dorothy.

"Because if you did not wear spectacles the brightness and glory of the Emerald City would blind you. Even those who live in the City must wear spectacles night and day. They are all locked on, for Oz so ordered it when the City was first built, and I have the only key that will unlock them."

He opened the big box, and Dorothy saw that it was filled with spectacles of every size and shape. All of them had green glasses in them. The Guardian of the Gates found a pair that would just fit Dorothy and put them over her eyes. There were two golden bands fastened to them that passed around the back of her head, where they were locked together by a little key that was at the end of a chain the Guardian of the Gates wore around his neck. When they were on, Dorothy could not take them off had she wished, but of course she did not wish to be blinded by the glare of the Emerald City, so she said nothing.

Then the green man fitted spectacles for the Scarecrow and the Tin Woman and the Lioness, and even on little Toto; and all were locked fast with the key.

Then the Guardian of the Gates put on his own glasses and told them he was ready to show them to the Palace. Taking a big golden key from a peg on the wall, he opened another gate, and they all followed him through the portal into the streets of the Emerald City.

CHAPTER XI

The Wonderful City of Oz

Even with eyes protected by the green spectacles, Dorothy and her friends were at first dazzled by the brilliancy of the wonderful City. The streets were lined with beautiful houses all built of green marble and studded everywhere with sparkling emeralds. They walked over a pavement of the same green marble, and where the blocks were joined together were rows of emeralds, set closely, and glittering in the brightness of the sun. The window panes were of green glass; even the sky above the City had a green tint, and the rays of the sun were green.

There were many NPCs—men, women, and children—walking about, and these were all dressed in green clothes and had greenish skin. They looked at Dorothy and her strangely assorted company with wondering eyes, and the children all ran away and hid behind their mothers when they saw the Lioness; but no one spoke to them. Many shops stood in the street, and Dorothy saw that everything in them was green. Green candy and green popcorn were offered for sale, as well as green shoes, green hats, and green clothes of all sorts. At one place a man was selling green lemonade, and when the children bought it Dorothy could see that they paid for it with green pennies.

"Shall we check the shops to see if they have any spells I could buy?" wondered Dorothy.

Scarecrow nodded eagerly. "Or magic items."

"But we have no money to buy them with," the Tin Woman pointed out.

"I'm sure those gems were evil," muttered Lioness.

There seemed to be no horses nor animals of any kind; the men carried things around in little green carts, which they pushed before them. Everyone seemed happy and contented and prosperous.

The Guardian of the Gates led them through the streets until they came to a big building, exactly in the middle of the City, which was the Palace of Oz, the Great Wizard. There was a soldier before the door, dressed in a green uniform and wearing a long green beard.

"Here are strangers," said the Guardian of the Gates to him, "and they demand to see the Great Oz."

"Step inside," answered the soldier, "and I will carry your message to him."

So they passed through the Palace Gates and were led into a big room with a green carpet and lovely green furniture set with emeralds. Both Dorothy and Scarecrow gave the jewels an appraising look, then shared a glance.

The soldier made them all wipe their feet upon a green mat before entering this room, and when they were seated he said politely:

"Please make yourselves comfortable while I go to the door of the Throne Room and tell Oz you are here."

"What a marvelous tapestry." Scarecrow took the Tin Woman's arm and turned her to face the wall.

Dorothy moved towards a delicate chair whose leather covering was fastened down with pins whose heads were emeralds. Taking a seat she pulled and twisted at them to no avail. As she weighed up the possible consequences of risking casting a *Magic Missile* in order to try to dislodge an emerald, the soldier returned. Hurriedly, Dorothy stood up and asked:

"Have you seen Oz?"

"Oh, no," returned the soldier; "I have never seen him. But I spoke to him as he sat behind his screen and gave him your message. He said he will grant you an audience, if you so desire; but each one of you must enter his presence alone, and he will admit but one each day. Therefore, as you must remain in the Palace for several days, I will have you shown to rooms where you may rest in comfort after your journey."

"Thank you," replied the girl; "that is very kind of Oz."

The soldier now blew upon a green whistle, and at once a young girl, dressed in a pretty green silk gown, entered the room. She had lovely green hair and green eyes, and she bowed low before Dorothy as she said, "Follow me and I will show you your room."

So Dorothy said good-bye to all her friends except Toto, and taking the dog in her arms followed the green girl through seven passages and up three flights of stairs until they came to a room at the front of the Palace. It was the sweetest little room in the world, with a soft comfortable bed that had sheets of green silk and a green velvet counterpane. There was a tiny fountain in the middle of the room, that shot a spray of green perfume into the air, to fall back into a beautifully carved green marble basin. Beautiful green flowers stood in the windows, and there was a shelf with a row of little green books. When Dorothy had time to open these books she was disappointed not to come across any new spells, but found them full of absurd green pictures that made her laugh, they were so funny.

In a wardrobe were many green dresses, made of silk and satin and velvet; and all of them fitted Dorothy exactly. A *Detect Magic*, however, revealed nothing unusual about them.

"Make yourself perfectly at home," said the green girl, "and if you wish for anything ring the bell. Oz will send for you tomorrow morning."

She left Dorothy alone and went back to the others. These she also led to rooms, and each one of them found themselves lodged in a very pleasant part of the Palace. Of course this politeness was wasted on the Scarecrow; for when he found himself alone in his room he stood stupidly in one spot, just within the doorway, to wait till morning. It would not rest him to lie down, and he could not close his eyes; so he remained all night staring at a little spider which was weaving its web in a corner of the room, just as if it were not one of the most wonderful rooms in the world.

The Tin Woman lay down on her bed from force of habit, for she remembered when she was made of flesh; but not being able to sleep, she passed the night moving her joints up and down to make sure they kept in good working order. The Lioness would have preferred a bed of dried leaves in the forest, and did not like being shut up in a room; but she had too much sense to let this worry her, so she sprang upon the bed and rolled herself up like a cat and purred herself asleep in a minute.

The next morning, after breakfast, the green maiden came to fetch Dorothy, and suggested the young Sorceress dress in a gown made of green brocaded satin. Dorothy also put on a green silk apron and tied a green ribbon around Toto's neck, and they started for the Throne Room of the Great Oz.

First they came to a great hall in which were many ladies and gentlemen of the court, all dressed in rich costumes. These NPCs had nothing to do but talk to each other, but they always came to wait outside the Throne Room every morning, although they were never permitted to see Oz. As Dorothy entered they looked at her curiously, and one of them whispered:

"Are you really going to look upon the face of Oz the Terrible?"

"Of course," answered the girl, "if he will see me."

"Oh, he will see you," said the soldier who had taken her message to the Wizard, "although he does not like to have people ask to see him. Indeed, at first he was angry and said I should send you back where you came from. Then he asked me what you looked like, and when I mentioned your silver shoes he was very much interested. At last I told him about the mark upon your forehead, and he decided he would admit you to his presence."

Just then a bell rang, and the green girl said to Dorothy, "That is the signal. You must go into the Throne Room alone."

She opened a little door and Dorothy walked boldly through and found herself in a wonderful place. It was a big, round room with a high arched roof, and the walls and ceiling and floor were covered with large emeralds set closely together. In the center of the roof was a great light, as bright as the sun, which made the emeralds sparkle in a wonderful manner.

But what interested Dorothy most was the big throne of green marble that stood in the middle of the room. It was shaped like a chair and sparkled with gems, as did everything else. In the center of the chair was an enormous Head, without a body to support it or any arms or legs whatsoever. There was no hair upon this Head, but it had eyes and a nose and mouth, and was much bigger than the head of the biggest giant.

As Dorothy gazed upon this in wonder and fear, the eyes turned slowly and looked at her sharply and steadily. Then the mouth moved, and Dorothy heard a voice say:

"I am Oz, the Great and Terrible. Who are you, and why do you seek me?"

It was not such an awful voice as she had expected to come from the big Head; so she took courage and answered:

"I am Dorothy, the Small and Meek. I have come to you for help."

The eyes looked at her thoughtfully for a full minute. Then said the voice:

"Where did you get the Silver Shoes?"

"I got them from the Wicked Witch of the East, when my house fell on her and killed her," she replied.

"Where did you get the mark upon your forehead?" continued the voice.

"That is where the Good Witch of the North kissed me when she bade me good-bye and sent me to you with a *Protection from Evil*," said the girl.

Again the eyes looked at her sharply, and they seemed to accept she was telling the truth. For Oz then asked in a more conciliatory tone, "What do you wish me to do?"

"*Teleport* me back to Kansas, where my Aunt Em and Uncle Henry are," she answered earnestly. "Although your country is so beautiful and full of interesting adventures, mobs and treasure, I am sure Aunt Em will be dreadfully worried over my being away so long."

The eyes winked three times, and then they turned up to the ceiling and down to the floor and rolled around so queerly that they seemed to see every part of the room. And at last they looked at Dorothy again.

"Why should I do this for you?" asked Oz.

"Because you are level fifteen and must surely have the *Teleport* spell; because you are a Great Wizard and although I have reached level eight, most of my skills are still at their level one cap."

"But you were strong enough to kill the Wicked Witch of the East," said Oz.

"That was extraordinary luck," returned Dorothy simply; "I could not help it."

"Well," said the Head, "I will give you my answer. You have no right to expect me to *Teleport* you back to Kansas unless you do something for me in return. In this country everyone must pay for everything he gets. If you wish me to use my magic power to send you home again you must do something for me first. Help me and I will help you."

"What must I do?" asked the girl.

"Kill the Wicked Witch of the West," answered Oz.

"But I cannot!" exclaimed Dorothy, greatly surprised. "I might be level eight, but I've only got five spells in my spell book."

"You killed the Witch of the East and you wear the Silver Shoes, which bear a powerful charm. There is now but one Wicked Witch left in all this land, and when you can tell me she is dead I will send you back to Kansas—but not before."

The little girl began to weep, she was so much disappointed; and the eyes winked again and looked upon her anxiously, as if the Great Oz was saying that he would help her if he could.

"I never had the opportunity to kill anything in Kanas," she sobbed. "And I'm so underpowered here for my level. Even if I wanted to, how could I kill the Wicked Witch? If you, who are Great and Terrible, cannot kill her yourself, how do you expect me to do it with only five spells?"

"I do not know," said the Head; "but that is my answer, and until the Wicked Witch dies you will not see your uncle and aunt again. Remember that the Witch is Wicked—tremendously Wicked—and ought to be killed. Now go, and do not ask to see me again until you have done your task."

Dorothy rallied herself and looked at the Head, whose eyes shifted away uneasily. "Can you at least give me more spells for my spellbook? You must have... oh... fifty, a hundred even, at your level. *Fireball*, *Lightning Bolt* and *Summon Monster IV* would all be very useful..."

"Stop! You have heard my instruction. Go now and ask for nothing until you have killed the Witch."

Sorrowfully Dorothy left the Throne Room and went back where the Lioness and the Scarecrow and the Tin Woman were waiting to hear what Oz had said to her. "There is no hope for me," she said sadly, "for Oz will not send me home until I have killed the Wicked Witch of the West; and that I can never do. I'm sure she's a boss fight that needs a whole raiding party."

Her friends were sorry, but could do nothing to help her; so Dorothy went to her own room and lay down on the bed and cried herself to sleep.

The next morning the soldier with the green whiskers came to the Scarecrow and said:

"Come with me, for Oz has sent for you."

So the Scarecrow followed him and was admitted into the great Throne Room, where he saw, sitting in the emerald throne, a most lovely Lady. She was dressed in green silk gauze and wore upon her flowing green locks a crown of jewels. Growing from her shoulders were wings, gorgeous in color and so light that they fluttered if the slightest breath of air reached them.

When the Scarecrow had bowed, as prettily as his straw stuffing would let him, before this beautiful creature, she looked upon him sweetly, and said:

"I am Oz, the Great and Terrible. Who are you, and why do you seek me?"

Now the Scarecrow, who had expected to see the great Head Dorothy had told him of, was much astonished; but he answered her bravely.

"I am only a Scarecrow, stuffed with straw. I have been *Cursed* and *Polymorphed*, and I come to you praying that you will restore my Intelligence so I can regain my Bard abilities. And while there are tactical advantages to being made of straw, I think I'd like to resume my body and be just like any other human male in your dominions."

93

"Why should I do this for you?" asked the Lady.

"Because you are wise and powerful, and no one else can help me," answered the Scarecrow.

"I never grant favors without some return," said Oz; "but this much I will promise. If you will kill for me the Wicked Witch of the West, I will bestow upon you a *Dispel Magic* to remove the curse, and moreover a *Headband of Intellect*, since even with your Bard abilities restored, you will want to avoid the penalties on certain skills that come with a low Intelligence."

"I thought you asked Dorothy to kill the Witch," said the Scarecrow, in surprise.

"So I did. I don't care who kills her. But until she is dead I will not grant your wish. Now go, and do not seek me again until you have earned the Intelligence you so greatly desire."

The Scarecrow went sorrowfully back to his friends and told them what Oz had said; and Dorothy was surprised to find that the Great Wizard was not a Head, as she had seen him, but a lovely Lady.

"All the same," said the Scarecrow, "she was unfriendly and thought only of killing the Witch."

On the next morning the soldier with the green whiskers came to the Tin Woman and said:

"Oz has sent for you. Follow me."

So the Tin Woman followed him and came to the great Throne Room. She did not know whether she would find Oz a lovely Lady or a Head, but she hoped it would be the lovely Lady.

94

"For," she said to herself, "if it is the Head, I am sure I shall not be given an *Atonement*, since a head has no sense of romance and therefore cannot feel for me. But if it is the lovely Lady I shall beg hard for an *Atonement*, for she is more likely to be kindly hearted."

But when the Tin Woman entered the great Throne Room she saw neither the Head nor the Lady, for Oz had taken the shape of a most terrible Beast. It was nearly as big as an elephant, and the green throne seemed hardly strong enough to hold its weight. The Beast had a head like that of a rhinoceros, only there were five eyes in its face. There were five long arms growing out of its body, and it also had five long, slim legs. Thick, woolly hair covered every part of it, and a more dreadful-looking monster could not be imagined. It was fortunate the Tin Woman had no heart at that moment, for it would have beat loud and fast from terror. But being only tin, the Tin Woman was not at all afraid, although she was much disappointed.

"I am Oz, the Great and Terrible," spoke the Beast, in a voice that was one great roar. "Who are you, and why do you seek me?"

"I am a Warrior, and made of tin. I lost my feeling of love and broke a young man's heart along with my Paladin Code of Conduct. I pray you to give me an *Atonement* so that I can restore my Paladin class."

"Why should I do this?" demanded the Beast.

"Because I ask it, and you are a ruler over divine casters who can grant my request," answered the Tin Woman.

Oz gave a low growl at this, but said, gruffly: "If you indeed desire an *Atonement*, you must earn it."

"How?" asked the Tin Woman.

"Help Dorothy to kill the Wicked Witch of the West," replied the Beast. "When the Witch is dead, come to me, and I will then make you the highest level and kindest Paladin in all the Land of Oz."

So the Tin Woman was forced to return sorrowfully to her friends and tell them of the terrible Beast she had seen. They all wondered greatly at the many forms the Great Wizard could take upon himself, and the Lioness said:

"If he is a Beast when I go to see him, I shall roar my loudest, and so frighten him that he will grant all I ask. And if he is the lovely Lady, I shall pretend to spring upon her, and so compel her to do my bidding. And if he is the great Head, he will be at my mercy; for I will roll this head all about the room until he promises to give us what we desire. So be of good cheer, my friends, for all will yet be well."

The next morning the soldier with the green whiskers led the Lioness to the great Throne Room and bade her enter the presence of Oz.

The Lioness at once passed through the door, and glancing around saw, to her surprise, that before the throne was a Ball of Fire, so fierce and glowing she could scarcely bear to gaze upon it. Her first thought was that Oz had by accident caught on fire and was burning up; but when she tried to go nearer, the heat was so intense that it singed her whiskers, and she crept back tremblingly to a spot nearer the door.

Then a low, quiet voice came from the Ball of Fire, and these were the words it spoke:

"I am Oz, the Great and Terrible. Who are you, and why do you seek me?"

And the Lioness answered, "I am a Cowardly Lioness, a Barbarian who cannot Rage. I came to you to beg that you give me back my ability to Rage, so that in reality I may become the Queen of Beasts, as men call me."

"Why should I restore your Rage?" demanded Oz.

"Because of all Wizards you are the greatest, and a *Dispel Magic* from you will have the power to grant my request," answered the Lioness.

The Ball of Fire burned fiercely for a time, and the voice said, "Bring me proof that the Wicked Witch is dead, and that moment I will give you back your Rage. But as long as the Witch lives, you must remain a Barbarian without your greatest ability."

The Lioness was angry at this speech, but could say nothing in reply, and while she stood silently gazing at the Ball of Fire it became so furiously hot that she turned tail and rushed from the room. She was glad to find her friends waiting for her, and told them of her terrible interview with the Wizard.

"What shall we do now?" asked Dorothy sadly.

"There is only one thing we can do," returned the Lioness, "and that is to go to the land of the Winkies, seek out the Wicked Witch, and destroy her."

"But suppose we cannot?" said the girl.

"Then I shall never be able to Rage," declared the Lioness.

"And I shall never have my Intelligence restored," added the Scarecrow.

"And I shall never be a Paladin again," spoke the Tin Woman.

"And I shall never see Aunt Em and Uncle Henry," said Dorothy, beginning to cry.

"Be careful!" cried the green girl. "The tears will fall on your green silk gown and spot it."

So Dorothy dried her eyes and said, "I suppose we must try it; but I am sure we are heading for a wipe and the quest will not prove worthwhile, even to see Aunt Em again."

"I will go with you; but without Rage, I won't be able to kill the Witch," said the Lioness.

"I will go too," declared the Scarecrow; "but I shall not be of much help to you without my Bard abilities, I am such a fool."

"I haven't the Paladin Code of Conduct to adhere to, yet it seems to me wrong to set out to harm anyone, even a Witch," remarked the Tin Woman; "but if you go I certainly shall go with you and if I happen to inadvertently share in XP and treasure from your wicked actions I shall at least be on hand to point out what a Lawful Good person should have done."

Therefore it was decided to start upon their journey the next morning, and the Tin Woman sharpened her axe on a green grindstone and had all her joints properly oiled. The Scarecrow stuffed himself with fresh straw and Dorothy put new paint on his eyes that he might see better. The green girl, who was very kind to them, filled Dorothy's basket with good things to eat, and fastened a little bell around Toto's neck with a green ribbon which he removed as soon as she had left. For much as he admired the pretty bell, alerting your enemies to your presence did not seem like a good idea to Toto.

They went to bed quite early and slept soundly until daylight, when they were awakened by the crowing of a green cock that lived in the backyard of the Palace, and the cackling of a hen that had laid a green egg.

Chapter XII

The Search for the Wicked Witch

The soldier with the green whiskers led them through the streets of the Emerald City until they reached the room where the Guardian of the Gates lived. This officer unlocked their spectacles to put them back in his great box, and then he politely opened the gate for our friends.

"Which road leads to the Wicked Witch of the West?" asked Dorothy.

"There is no road," answered the Guardian of the Gates. "No one ever wishes to go that way."

"How, then, are we to find her?" inquired the girl.

"That will be easy," replied the man, "for when she knows you are in the country of the Winkies she will find you, and make you all her slaves."

"Perhaps not," said the Scarecrow, "for we mean to destroy her."

"Oh, that is different," said the Guardian of the Gates. "No one has ever destroyed her before, so I naturally thought she would make slaves of you, as she has of the rest. But take care; for she is wicked and fierce, and may not allow you to destroy her. Keep to the West, where the sun sets, and you cannot fail to find her."

They thanked him and bade him good-bye, and turned toward the West, walking over fields of soft grass dotted here and there with daisies and buttercups. Dorothy still wore the pretty silk dress she had put on in the palace, but now, to her surprise, she found it was no longer green, but pure white.

The Emerald City was soon left far behind. As they advanced the ground became rougher and hillier, for there were no farms nor houses in this country of the West, and the ground was untilled.

In the afternoon the sun shone hot in their faces, for there were no trees to offer them shade; so that before night Dorothy and Toto and the Lioness were tired, and lay down upon the grass and fell asleep, with the Tin Woman and the Scarecrow keeping watch.

Now, the Wicked Witch of the West had but one eye, yet that was an *Eye of the Eagle*; it was as powerful as a telescope, and could see everywhere. So, as she sat in the door of her castle, she happened to look around and saw Dorothy lying asleep, with her friends all about her. They were a long distance off, but the Wicked Witch was angry to find them in her country; so she blew upon a silver whistle of *Monster Summoning V* that hung around her neck.

At once there came running to her from all directions a pack of great wolves. They had long legs and fierce eyes and sharp teeth.

101

"Go to those people," said the Witch, "and tear them to pieces."

"Are you not going to make them your slaves?" asked the leader of the wolves.

"No," she answered, "one is of tin, and one of straw; one is a girl and another a Lioness. None of them is fit to work, so you may tear them into small pieces."

"Very well," said the wolf, and he dashed away at full speed, followed by the others.

It was lucky the Scarecrow and the Tin Woman were wide awake and heard the wolves coming.

"I can tank these," said the Tin Woman, "my natural armor class and my damage shield are so high, they will only hurt me on a critical. So get behind me and I will meet them as they come."

"I'm useless," answered the Scarecrow miserably, "but I shall wake Dorothy and offer you all what encouragement I can without an actual magical performance."

No sooner had Dorothy been alerted to the crisis, than she cast *Haste* on the party. With Tin Woman on one side and the Lioness on the other (and Toto barking bravely), Dorothy and the Scarecrow were protected while forty wolves circled the them, growling and making feint attacks.

It was clear that the moment was coming in which all the wolves would charge. Dorothy's spell gems had been grayed out following the *Haste* but returned to active status just in time. As the wolves edged forward, she cast a *Stinking Cloud* between the

Lioness and the attackers, forcing the wolves on that side of the party to recoil or fall *Nauseated* if they failed their fortitude checks. The Scarecrow, having no need to breathe, dashed into the cloud and dropped heavy rocks on the stricken ones.

On the other side of the battle, the Tin Woman seized her axe, which she had made very sharp, and as the leader of the wolves came on the Tin Woman swung her arm and scored a critical hit, chopping the wolf's head from its body, so that it immediately died. As soon as she could raise her axe another wolf came up, and he also fell under the sharp edge of the Tin Woman's weapon.

Possessing as she did a maxed *Opportune Blow* skill, no wolf could pass by the Tin Woman without incurring an attack of opportunity, and with a run of perfectly placed blows, she intercepted the attackers before they could reach Dorothy.

As for the young Sorceress, she was calmly firing *Magic Missiles* as often as her spell gems allowed, emptying her mana bar but destroying those wolves that had skirted the *Stinking Cloud*.

Eventually, every wolf was dead.

You have killed 40 wolves!
+ 35,000 XP

"Halfway to level nine," Dorothy announced, pleased.

The Tin Woman put down her axe and sat beside the Scarecrow, saying, "It was a good fight, friend."

"Yes, although I'm a little disappointed with the loot, just this High-Quality Wolf Pelt."

Standing among all the dead wolves, Dorothy did not feel like breakfast, so they started again upon their journey.

Now this same morning the Wicked Witch came to the door of her castle and looked out with her *Eye of the Eagle*. She saw that the strangers were still traveling through her country. This made her angrier than before, and she blew her silver whistle of *Monster Summoning V* again.

Straightaway a great flock of wild crows came flying toward her, enough to darken the sky.

And the Wicked Witch said to the King Crow, "Fly at once to the strangers; peck out their eyes and tear them to pieces."

The wild crows flew in one great flock toward Dorothy and her companions. When the little girl saw them coming she was afraid. "Tin Woman, you will never be able to intercept all these."

But the Scarecrow said, "This is my battle, so cast *Haste* then lie down beside me and you will not be harmed."

So as soon as Dorothy was done, they all lay upon the ground except the Scarecrow, and he stood up and stretched out his arms. And when the crows saw him they were frightened, as these birds always are by scarecrows, and did not dare to come any nearer. But the King Crow said:

"It is only a stuffed man. I will peck his eyes out."

The King Crow flew at the Scarecrow and managed a triple attack into Scarecrows eyes, which would have blinded any normal character. Scarecrow, however, reached up unperturbed, caught the bird by the head and twisted its neck until it died. And then the other crows flew at him, but their pecks were largely ineffectual, for the Scarecrow could not bleed. There were forty crows, and forty times the Scarecrow twisted a neck, until at last all were lying dead beside him. Then he called to his companions to rise, and again they went upon their journey.

You have killed 39 giant crows and King Crow!

+ 41,500 XP

"Some good XP there," announced Scarecrow, "but once again, no loot to speak of."

"Eighty percent of the way to level nine," said Dorothy cheerfully. "There's a lot to be said for being made of straw. That's a nice exploit."

When the Wicked Witch looked out again and saw all her crows lying in a heap, she got into a terrible rage, and blew again upon her silver whistle of *Monster Summoning V*.

Forthwith there was heard a great buzzing in the air, and a swarm of black bees came flying toward her.

"Go to the strangers and sting them to death!" commanded the Witch, and the bees turned and flew rapidly until they came to where Dorothy and her friends were walking. But the Tin Woman had seen them coming, and the Scarecrow had decided what to do.

"Take out my straw and scatter it over the little girl and the dog and the Lioness," he said to the Tin Woman, "and the bees cannot sting them."

"That is a foolish idea," said Dorothy, "you don't have enough straw in you and the bees would find a way through it. No, we had better *Hide*: that is, everyone but the Tin Woman who can stand in the open in that patch of sunlight and try to get the aggro."

The bees came and found Scarecrow, who had fumbled his *Hide* check. But no one else was visible except the bright, shining Tin Woman. The bees therefore rushed at the two figures, expending their stings uselessly on Scarecrow and breaking off all their stings against the armor of the Tin Woman, without hurting either of them at all. And as bees cannot live when their stings are gone that was the end of the black bees, and they lay scattered thick about the glade, like little heaps of fine coal.

You have killed 40 giant bees!
+ 44,000 XP

Then Dorothy, Toto and the Lioness came out of the bushes.

"Ding! I've reached Level Four in Warrior," said Tin Woman, "but I do wish we could have used that exploit to help me level in Paladin."

The Wicked Witch was so angry when she saw her black bees in little heaps like fine coal that she stamped her foot and tore her hair and gnashed her teeth. And then she called a dozen of her slaves, who were the Winkies, and gave them sharp spears, telling them to go to the strangers and destroy them.

The Winkies were not a brave people, but they had to do as they were told. So they marched away until they came near to

Dorothy. Then the Lioness gave a great roar and sprang towards them, and the poor Winkies were so frightened that they ran back as fast as they could.

"Oh," said Dorothy, disappointed, "I might have reached level nine if they had stayed for a fight."

When the Winkies returned to the castle the Wicked Witch beat them well with a strap, and sent them back to their work, after which she sat down to think what she should do next. She could not understand how all her plans to destroy these strangers had failed; but she was a powerful Witch, as well as a wicked one, and she soon made up her mind how to act.

There was, in her cupboard, a Golden Cap, with a circle of diamonds and rubies running round it. This Golden Cap had a charm. Whoever owned it could call three times upon the Winged Monkeys, who would obey any order they were given. But no person could command these strange creatures more than three times. Twice already the Wicked Witch had used the charm of the Cap. Once was when she had made the Winkies her slaves, and set herself to rule over their country. The Winged Monkeys had helped her do this. The second time was when she had fought against the Great Oz himself, and driven him out of the land of the West. The Winged Monkeys had also helped her in doing this. Only once more could she use this Golden Cap, for which reason she did not like to do so until all her other powers were exhausted. But now that the three daily usages of her silver whistle of *Monster Summoning V* were spent, and her slaves had been scared away by the Cowardly Lioness, she saw there was only one way left to destroy Dorothy and her friends.

So the Wicked Witch took the Golden Cap from her cupboard and placed it upon her head. Then she stood upon her left foot and said slowly:

"Ep-pe, pep-pe, kak-ke!"

Next she stood upon her right foot and said:

"Hil-lo, hol-lo, hel-lo!"

After this she stood upon both feet and cried in a loud voice:

"Ziz-zy, zuz-zy, zik!"

Now the charm began to work. The sky was darkened, and a low rumbling sound was heard in the air. There was a rushing of many wings, a great chattering and laughing, and the sun came out of the dark sky to show the Wicked Witch surrounded by a crowd of monkeys, each with a pair of immense and powerful wings on his shoulders.

One, much bigger than the others, seemed to be their leader. He flew close to the Witch and said, "You have called us for the third and last time. What do you command?"

"Go to the strangers who are within my land and destroy them all except the Lioness," said the Wicked Witch. "Bring that beast to me, for I have a mind to harness her like a horse, and make her work."

"Your commands shall be obeyed," said the leader. Then, with a great deal of chattering and noise, the Winged Monkeys flew away to the place where Dorothy and her friends were walking.

The attack of the Winged Monkeys was so swift that Dorothy barely had time to cast *Haste* before the monsters were on top of the party. Although the Tin Woman struck out as skillfully as ever, she was soon overwhelmed and having been grappled, was carried through the air until her captors were over a country thickly covered with sharp rocks. Here they dropped the poor Tin Woman, who fell a great distance to the rocks, where she lay so battered and dented that she could neither move nor groan.

Others of the Monkeys caught the Scarecrow, and with their long fingers pulled all of the straw out of his clothes and head. They made his hat and boots and clothes into a small bundle and threw it into the top branches of a tall tree.

The remaining Monkeys threw pieces of stout rope around the Lioness and wound many coils about her body and head and legs, until she was unable to bite or scratch or struggle in any way. Then they lifted her up and flew away with her to the Witch's castle, where she was placed in a small yard with a high iron fence around it, so that she could not escape.

But Dorothy they did not harm at all. She stood, with Toto in her arms, watching the sad fate of her comrades and thinking it would soon be her turn. The leader of the Winged Monkeys flew up to her, his long, hairy arms stretched out and his ugly face grinning terribly; but he saw the mark of the Good Witch's kiss upon her forehead and stopped short, motioning the others not to touch her.

"We cannot harm this little girl," he said to them, "for she has a *Protection from Evil* up, which prevents physical attacks upon her from summoned creatures. All we can do is to wrap these ropes around her and carry her to the castle of the Wicked Witch, where the Witch herself can kill her."

So, carefully and keeping their distance, they wove a net of ropes around Dorothy and carried her swiftly through the air until they came to the castle, where they set her down upon the front doorstep. Then the leader said to the Witch:

"We have obeyed you as far as we were able. The Tin Woman and the Scarecrow are destroyed, and the Lioness is tied up in your yard. The little girl we cannot harm directly, nor the dog she carries in her arms. Your power over our band is now ended, and you will never see us again."

Then all the Winged Monkeys, with much laughing and chattering and noise, flew into the air and were soon out of sight.

The Wicked Witch was both surprised and worried when she saw the mark on Dorothy's forehead, for although it was a secret to all but her sister Witches, she herself was a summoned creature, conjured to Oz from The Abyss. She looked down at Dorothy's feet, and seeing the Silver Shoes, began to tremble with fear, for she knew that this must be the slayer of the Wicked Witch of the East.

At first the Witch was tempted to run away from Dorothy; but she happened to look into the child's eyes and saw how simple the soul behind them was. Moreover, the little girl did not con red. In fact, she was only light blue, probably level eight. So the Wicked Witch laughed to herself, and thought, *I can still make her my slave.* Then she said to Dorothy, harshly and severely:

"Come with me; and see that you mind everything I tell you, for if you do not I will make an end of you, as I did of the Tin Woman and the Scarecrow."

Dorothy followed her through many of the beautiful rooms in her castle until they came to the kitchen, where the Witch bade her clean the pots and kettles and sweep the floor and keep the fire fed with wood.

Dorothy went to work meekly, with her mind made up to work as hard as she could; for she was glad the Wicked Witch had decided not to kill her.

With Dorothy hard at work, the Witch thought she would go into the courtyard and harness the Cowardly Lioness like a horse; it would amuse her, she was sure, to make the Lioness draw her chariot whenever she wished to go to drive. But as she opened the gate the Lioness gave a loud roar and bounded at her so fiercely that the Witch was afraid, and ran out and shut the gate again.

"If I cannot harness you," said the Witch to the Lioness, speaking through the bars of the gate, "I can starve you. You shall have nothing to eat until you do as I wish."

So after that she took no food to the imprisoned Lioness; but every day she came to the gate at noon and asked, "Are you ready to be harnessed like a horse?"

And the Lioness would answer, "No. If you come in this yard, I will bite you."

The reason the Lioness did not have to do as the Witch wished was that every night, while the Witch was asleep, Dorothy carried her food from the cupboard. After she had eaten she would lie down on her bed of straw, and Dorothy would lie beside her and put her head on the Lioness's soft fur while they talked of their troubles and tried to plan some way to escape. But they could find no way to get out of the castle, for it was constantly guarded by the yellow Winkies, who were the slaves of the Wicked Witch and too afraid of her not to do as she told them.

The girl had to work hard during the day, and often the Witch threatened to beat her with the same old broom she always carried in her hand. But, in truth, she simply could not strike Dorothy, because of the *Protection from Evil* provided by the mark upon her forehead. The child did not know this, and was full of fear for herself and Toto. Once the Witch struck Toto a blow with her broom and the brave little dog flew at her and bit her leg in return. The Witch did not bleed where she was bitten, for she was inhuman, and she shot Dorothy an anxious glance until reassured that the girl had not spotted the clue to the Witch's true demonic nature.

Dorothy's life became very sad as she grew to understand that it would be harder than ever to get back to Kansas and Aunt Em again. Sometimes she would cry bitterly for hours, with Toto sitting at her feet and looking into her face, whining dismally to show how sorry he was for his little mistress. Toto did not really care whether he was in Kansas or the Land of Oz so long as Dorothy was with him; but he knew the little girl was unhappy, and that made him unhappy too.

Now the Wicked Witch had a great longing to have for her own the Silver Shoes which the girl always wore. Her bees and her crows and her wolves were lying in heaps and drying up, and she had used up all the power of the Golden Cap; but if she could only get hold of the Silver Shoes, they would give her more power than all the other magic she had lost.

The difficulty for the Witch was that ever since Dorothy had attuned the magic shoes to her, they had become No Trade. No other player or NPC could use them unless Dorothy opted to un-attune them.

But the wicked creature was very cunning, and she finally thought of a trick that would give her what she wanted. She trapped Toto in a large laundry basket and called Dorothy over.

"I may not be able to harm you, but I can kill your familiar."

Toto, having been barking as loudly as he could, seemed to understand the threat, for he began to scrabble inside the basket and was now whining.

"Don't you dare hurt poor Toto! Let him go!"

The wicked woman, who was sitting on the basket, was greatly pleased with the success of her trick, and just laughed.

"You have until this time tomorrow to unattune those Silver Shoes and hand them over, or I will throw your familiar down the well and drown him.

"You are a wicked creature!" cried Dorothy. And she ran to her room in great distress. Was there nothing she could do but hand over the Silver Shoes? That night she crept across the courtyard with as basket of food for Lioness and explained her woes.

The Cowardly Lioness nuzzled Dorothy to comfort her and then said, "I do not know if this is any help, but I have noticed that the Winkies never enter the small tower in the corner there. They avoid it. Perhaps you should see why."

"I will," said Dorothy, without much hope. But she immediately walked quietly across the cobbles to where a wooden door stood closed with a sign upon it.

Anyone opening this door will be struck by a terrible *Curse*!

Dorothy looked at the door with a sense of skepticism. It could possibly be that a *Glyph of Warding* was present, but did the Witch even have that spell? Then she cast *Detect Magic*. There was none. As she had guessed, the sign was a bluff, perfectly adequate to keep the Winkies away. But there was no *Glyph of Warding* or other magical trap that cast a *Curse* spell.

All the same, Dorothy flinched slightly as she opened the door and stepped into the tower. After she was safely on the inside, with increasing confidence and a growing curiosity, she climbed the curving steps to the top room of the tower, where she found a door that was open and beyond it a remarkable room lit by moonlight.

114

A summoning pentacle was on the floor, nearby was a lectern with a spell book (a spell book!) and the remains of burned-out candles were everywhere. Behind the lectern were shelves with mysterious jars and items such as the skull of a goat. Casting *Detect Magic* again and finding only a faint residue of magic present, Dorothy stepped carefully into the room and went to the book.

It was open but the words were completely mysterious, made from fanciful letters that Dorothy had never seen before. They made sense, though, as soon as she cast her *Read Magic* spell. For the words on the page rearranged themselves to describe the steps to be taken by a wizard in order to cast *Summon Demon*.

Revelation came to Dorothy. The Wicked Witch of the West was a summoned demon. That explained why she couldn't hurt Dorothy, not while the *Protection from Evil* was surrounding her. And reading on, Dorothy found the section that confirmed her insight.

Demon of the Abyss (Witch)
Witch level 10
HP 98   Mana 144
Str 9
Int 17
Wis 9
Con 14
Dex 10
Cha 6

Damage Resistance 10 vs cold iron or good opponents

Immunities: electricity, poison

Resistances: acid 10, cold 10, fire 10.

Abilities: *See Invisible, Darkness, Dispel Magic*

Skills: Perception +20; Sleight of Hand +12; Stealth +8.

Spells: level 1 x 5; level 2 x 4; level 3 x 4; level 4 x 3;

level 5 x 2.

A Demon of the Abyss (Witch) has no need for a spell book and can slot any new spell of her choosing each night at midnight.

A Demon of the Abyss (Witch) always makes great effort to hide her true nature, for she has a weakness. If touched by quicksilver she is immediately expelled from the Prime plane and cast once more into the chaos of the Abyss, never to return for at least a hundred and one years.

Quicksilver? Dorothy searched among the bottles of the shelves until she found a small vial containing and shiny, liquid metal that did, indeed, look like silver. The label on the vial was "Mercury" and Dorothy remembered that this was another name for quicksilver. Feeling elated that she might have found a way to save Toto, Dorothy placed the tightly stoppered vial carefully in the right pocket of her dress.

The rest of the night, Dorothy spent transcribing spells from the spell book on the lectern into her own spell book, until dawn came, when—although tired—she marched out of the tower feeling like a genuine level 8 Sorceress, with her gem slots containing: *Magic Missile, Jump, Feather Fall*, and *Shield* for her first level spells; *Stinking Cloud, Web*, and *Mage Armor* for her second; *Fireball* and *Haste* for her third and *Summon Monster IV* for her fourth.

When the Wicked Witch rang for her breakfast, Dorothy took up a tray, with a bowl of mercury hidden under a silver lid.

"There you are at last, you lazy girl. Are you ready to unattune my Silver Slippers and hand them over?" The Witch gestured towards where Toto was tied tight to the bedpost and gave a cruel smile.

"I will, after I've given you your breakfast." Heart beating fast, for a demon with level five spells was a terribly dangerous opponent should something go wrong, Dorothy set the tray down in such a way that her body shielded it. Then she took off the lid, carefully lifted the bowl in both hands, came close enough that she couldn't possibly miss, and threw the mercury over the Witch's face and neck.

"No!" the Witch screamed in surprise and horror as steam began to pour from her body. "How did you know quicksilver would be the end of me?"

"I read the book in the tower," answered Dorothy.

"Well, in a few minutes I shall be all melted, and you will have the castle to yourself. I have been wicked in my day, but I never thought a little girl like you would ever be able to melt me and end my wicked deeds. Look out—here I go!"

With these words the Witch fell down in a brown, melted, shapeless mass and began to spread over the bedspread. Seeing that she had really melted away to nothing, Dorothy shook the last few drops of mercury over the mess. She then hurried to free Toto, who jumped into her arms, licking her face eagerly.

You have slain the Wicked Witch of the East!

Exp gain 140,000.

You are now level 9.

You have 1 Attribute point to spend. You have 3 Skill points to spend.

You have unlocked level 5 Spells.

You may now cast:

5 level 1 Spells

3 level 2 Spells

2 level 3 Spells

2 level 4 Spells

1 level 5 Spell

It seemed clear to Dorothy that the Attribute point should be assigned to Intelligence, to increase her mana pool.

```
Dorothy, level 9 Sorceress

HP 49    Mana 108

Str 7

Int 16

Wis 11

Con 7

Dex 7

Cha 13
```

Next, being at last free to do as she chose, she ran out to the courtyard to tell the Lioness that the Wicked Witch of the West had come to an end, and that they were no longer prisoners in a strange land.

CHAPTER XIII

The Rescue

The Cowardly Lioness was much pleased to hear that the Wicked Witch had been melted by a bowl of quicksilver, and Dorothy at once unlocked the gate of her prison and set her free. They went in together to the castle, where Dorothy's first act was to call all the Winkies together and tell them that they were no longer slaves.

There was great rejoicing among the yellow Winkies, for they had been made to work hard during many years for the Wicked Witch, who had always treated them with great cruelty. They kept this day as a holiday, then and ever after, and spent the time in feasting and dancing.

"If our friends, the Scarecrow and the Tin Woman, were only with us," said the Lioness, "I should be quite happy."

"Don't you suppose we could rescue them?" asked the girl anxiously.

"We can try," answered the Lioness.

So they called the yellow Winkies and asked them if they would help to rescue their friends, and the Winkies said that they would be delighted to do all in their power for Dorothy, who had set them free from bondage. She chose a number of the Winkies from those who were at least level 1, and they all started away. They traveled that day and part of the next until they came to the rocky plain where the Tin Woman lay, all battered and bent. Her axe was near her, but the blade was rusted and the handle broken off short.

The Winkies lifted her tenderly in their arms, and carried her back to the Yellow Castle again, Dorothy shedding a few tears by the way at the sad plight of her old friend, and the Lioness looking sober and sorry. When they reached the castle Dorothy said to the Winkies:

"Are any of your people tinsmiths?"

"Oh, yes. Some of us are very good tinsmiths," they told her.

"Then bring them to me," she said. And when the tinsmiths came, bringing with them all their tools in baskets, she inquired, "Can you straighten out those dents in the Tin Woman, and bend her back into shape again, and solder her together where she is broken?"

The tinsmiths looked the Tin Woman over carefully and then answered that they thought they could mend her so she would be as good as ever. So they set to work in one of the big yellow rooms of the castle and worked for three days and four nights, hammering and twisting and bending and soldering and polishing and pounding at the legs and body and head of the Tin Woman, until at last she was straightened out into her old form, and her joints worked as well as ever. To be sure, there were several patches on

121

her, but the tinsmiths did a good job, and as the Tin Woman was not a vain woman she did not mind the patches at all.

When, at last, she walked into Dorothy's room and thanked her for being rescued, she was so pleased that she wept tears of joy, and Dorothy had to wipe every tear carefully from her face with her apron, so her joints would not be rusted. At the same time Dorothy's own tears fell thick and fast at the joy of meeting her old friend again, and these tears did not need to be wiped away. As for the Lioness, she wiped her eyes so often with the tip of her tail that it became quite wet, and she was obliged to go out into the courtyard and hold it in the sun till it dried.

"If we only had the Scarecrow with us again," said the Tin Woman, when Dorothy had finished telling her everything that had happened, "I should be quite happy."

"We must try to find him," said the girl.

So she called the Winkies to help her, and they walked all that day and part of the next until they came to the tall tree in the branches of which the Winged Monkeys had tossed the Scarecrow's clothes.

It was a very tall tree, and the trunk was so smooth that no one could climb it; but the Tin Woman said at once, "I'll chop it down, and then we can get the Scarecrow's clothes."

Now while the tinsmiths had been at work mending the Tin Woman herself, another of the Winkies, who was a goldsmith, had made an axe-handle of solid gold and fitted it to the Tin Woman's axe, instead of the old broken handle. Others polished the blade until all the rust was removed and it glistened like burnished silver. A grandmaster tinsmith then added the Eversharp condition.

As soon as she had spoken, the Tin Woman began to chop, and in a short time the tree fell over with a crash, whereupon the Scarecrow's clothes fell out of the branches and rolled off on the ground.

Dorothy picked them up and had the Winkies carry them back to the castle, where they were stuffed with nice, clean straw: and behold! Here was the Scarecrow, as good as ever, thanking them over and over again for saving him.

Now that they were reunited, Dorothy reformed the party group and her friends spent a few happy days at the Yellow Castle, where they found everything they needed to make them comfortable.

But one day the girl thought of Aunt Em, and said, "We must go back to Oz, and claim his promise."

"Yes," said the Tin Woman, "at last I shall get my Paladin class restored."

"And I shall get my Intelligence," added the Scarecrow joyfully.

"And I shall get my Rage," said the Lioness thoughtfully.

"And I shall get back to Kansas," cried Dorothy, clapping her hands. "Oh, let us start for the Emerald City tomorrow!"

This they decided to do. The next day they called the Winkies together and bade them good-bye. The Winkies were sorry to

123

have them go, and they had grown so fond of the Tin Woman that they begged her to stay and rule over them and the Yellow Land of the West. Finding they were determined to go, the Winkies gave Toto and the Lioness each a golden collar of +2 Charisma; and to Dorothy they presented a beautiful bracelet studded with diamonds with a + 2 Armor Class bonus; and to the Scarecrow they gave a gold-headed Walking Stick of +5 Acrobatics, to keep him from stumbling; and to the Tin Woman they offered a silver oil-can, inlaid with gold and set with precious jewels and filled with *Oil of Evasion*.

Every one of the travelers made the Winkies a pretty speech in return, and all shook hands with them until their arms ached.

Dorothy went to the Witch's cupboard to fill her basket with food for the journey, and there she saw a Golden Cap. She tried it on her own head and found that it fitted her exactly. She did not know anything about the charm of the Golden Cap, but after casting *Detect Magic* she knew that it was powerful, so she made up her mind to wear it and carry her sunbonnet in the basket.

It was very tempting to bring the spell book from the tower, which was worth a great deal of gold. But having made copies of all the spells it contained into her own UI spell book, there was no need to carry such a large tome around with her and it would have made her Encumbered. Reluctantly, then, Dorothy left the book in the tower, having first made the Winkies promise not to move it.

Then, being prepared for the journey, they all started for the Emerald City; and the Winkies gave them three cheers and many good wishes to carry with them.

CHAPTER XIV

The Winged Monkeys

You will remember there was no road—not even a pathway—between the castle of the Wicked Witch and the Emerald City. When the four travelers went in search of the Witch she had seen them coming, and so sent the Winged Monkeys to bring them to her. It was much harder to find their way back through the big fields of buttercups and yellow daisies than it was being carried. They knew, of course, they must go straight east, toward the rising sun; and they started off in the right way. But at noon, when the sun was over their heads, they did not know which was east and which was west, and that was the reason they were lost in the great fields. They kept on walking, however, and at night the moon came out and shone brightly. So they lay down among the sweet smelling yellow flowers and slept soundly until morning: all but the Scarecrow and the Tin Woman.

The next morning the sun was behind a cloud, but they started on as if they were quite sure which way they were going.

"If we walk far enough," said Dorothy, "I am sure we shall sometime come to some place."

But day by day passed away, and they still saw nothing before them but the scarlet fields. The Scarecrow began to grumble a bit.

"We have surely lost our way," he said, "and unless we find it again in time to reach the Emerald City, I shall never get my Intelligence."

"Nor I my Paladin class," declared the Tin Woman. "It seems to me I can scarcely wait till I get to Oz for our reward, and you must admit this is a very long journey."

"You see," said the Cowardly Lioness, with a whimper, "I haven't the benefits of Rage to keep tramping forever, without getting anywhere at all."

Then Dorothy lost heart. She sat down on the grass and looked at her companions, and they sat down and looked at her, and Toto found that for the first time in his life he was too tired to chase a butterfly that flew past his head. So he put out his tongue and panted and looked at Dorothy as if to ask what they should do next.

"Suppose we call the field mice," she suggested. "They could probably tell us the way to the Emerald City."

"To be sure they could," cried the Scarecrow. "Why didn't we think of that before?"

Dorothy blew the little whistle she had always carried about her neck since the Queen of the Mice had given it to her. In a few minutes they heard the pattering of tiny feet, and many of the small gray mice came running up to her. Among them was the Queen herself, who asked, in her squeaky little voice:

"What can I do for my friends?"

"We have lost our way," said Dorothy. "Can you tell us where the Emerald City is?"

"Certainly," answered the Queen; "but it is a great way off, for you have had it at your backs all this time." Then she noticed Dorothy's Golden Cap, and said, "Why don't you use the charm of the Cap, and call the Winged Monkeys to you? They will carry you to the City of Oz in less than an hour."

"I didn't know there was a charm," answered Dorothy, in surprise. "What is it?"

"It is written inside the Golden Cap," replied the Queen of the Mice. "But if you are going to call the Winged Monkeys we must run away, for they are full of mischief and think it great fun to plague us."

"Won't they hurt me?" asked the girl anxiously.

"Oh, no. They must obey the wearer of the Cap. Good-bye!" And she scampered out of sight, with all the mice hurrying after her.

Dorothy looked inside the Golden Cap and saw some strange letters written upon the lining. These, she thought, must be the charm, so she cast *Read Magic*, studied the directions carefully and put the Cap upon her head.

"Ep-pe, pep-pe, kak-ke!" she said, standing on her left foot.

"What did you say?" asked the Scarecrow, who did not know what she was doing.

128

"Hil-lo, hol-lo, hel-lo!" Dorothy went on, standing this time on her right foot.

"Hello!" replied the Tin Woman calmly.

"Ziz-zy, zuz-zy, zik!" said Dorothy, who was now standing on both feet. This ended the saying of the charm, and they heard a great chattering and flapping of wings, as the band of Winged Monkeys flew up to them.

The King bowed low before Dorothy, and asked, "What is your command?"

"We wish to go to the Emerald City," said the child, "and we have lost our way."

"We will carry you," replied the King, and no sooner had he spoken than two of the Monkeys caught Dorothy in their arms and flew away with her. Others took the Scarecrow and the Tin Woman and the Lioness, and one little Monkey seized Toto and flew after them, although the dog tried hard to bite him.

The Scarecrow and the Tin Woman were rather frightened at first, for they remembered how badly the Winged Monkeys had treated them before; but they saw that no harm was intended, so they rode through the air quite cheerfully, and had a fine time looking at the pretty gardens and woods far below them.

Dorothy found herself riding easily between two of the biggest Monkeys, one of them the King himself. They had made a chair of their hands and were careful not to hurt her.

"Why do you have to obey the charm of the Golden Cap?" she asked.

"That is a long story," answered the King, with a winged laugh; "but as we have a long journey before us, I will pass the time by telling you about it, if you wish."

"I shall be glad to hear it," she replied.

"Once," began the leader, "we were a free people, living happily in a great forest, flying from tree to tree, eating nuts and fruit, and doing just as we pleased without calling anybody master. Perhaps some of us were rather too full of mischief at times, flying down to pull the tails of the animals that had no wings, chasing birds, and throwing nuts at the people who walked in the forest. But we were careless and happy and full of fun, and enjoyed every minute of the day. This was many years ago, in a plane adjacent to the Plane of Air.

"There lived here then, away at the North, a beautiful princess, who was also a powerful sorceress, level eight. All her magic was used to help the people, and she was never known to hurt anyone who was good. Her name was Gayelette, and she lived in a handsome palace built from great blocks of ruby. Everyone loved her, but her greatest sorrow was that she could find no one to love in return, since all the men were much too stupid and ugly to mate with one so beautiful and wise. At last, however, she found a boy who was handsome and manly and wise beyond his years. Gayelette made up her mind that when he grew to be a man she would make him her husband, so she took him to her ruby palace and used all her magic powers to make him as strong and good and lovely as any woman could wish. When he grew to manhood,

Quelala, as he was called, was said to be the best and wisest man in all the land, while his manly beauty was so great that Gayelette loved him dearly, and hastened to make everything ready for the wedding.

"My grandfather was at that time the King of the Winged Monkeys which lived in the forest near Gayelette's palace, and the old fellow loved a joke better than a good dinner. One day, just before the wedding, my grandfather was flying out with his band when he saw Quelala walking beside the river. The soon-to-be prince was dressed in a foolish and self-important costume of pink silk and purple velvet, and my grandfather thought he would see what he could do. At his word the band flew down and seized Quelala, carried him in their arms until they were over the middle of the river, and then dropped him into the water.

"'Swim out, my fine fellow,' cried my grandfather, 'and see if the water has spotted your clothes.' Quelala was not in the least spoiled by all his good fortune. He laughed, when he came to the top of the water, and swam in to shore. But when Gayelette came running out to him she found his silks and velvet all ruined by the river.

"The princess was angry, and she knew, of course, who did it. She had all the Winged Monkeys brought before her, and she said at first that their wings should be tied and they should be treated as they had treated Quelala, and dropped in the river. But my grandfather pleaded hard, for he knew the Monkeys would drown in the river with their wings tied, and Quelala said a kind word for them also; so that Gayelette finally spared them, on condition that the Winged Monkeys should ever after do three times the bidding of the owner of the Golden Cap. This Cap had been made for a wedding present to Quelala, and it is said to have cost the princess half her kingdom. Of course my grandfather and all the other Monkeys at once agreed to the condition, and that is how it happens that we are three times the slaves of the owner of the Golden Cap, whosoever he may be."

"And what became of them?" asked Dorothy, who had been greatly interested in the story.

"Quelala being the first owner of the Golden Cap," replied the Monkey, "he was the first to lay his wishes upon us. As his bride could not bear the sight of us, he called us all to him in the forest after he had married her and ordered us always to keep where she could never again set eyes on a Winged Monkey, which we were glad to do, for we were all afraid of her.

"This was all we ever had to do until the Golden Cap fell into the hands of the Wicked Witch of the West, who made us enslave the Winkies, and afterward drive Oz himself out of the Land of the West. Now the Golden Cap is yours, and three times you have the right to lay your wishes upon us."

As the Monkey King finished his story Dorothy looked down and saw the green, shining walls of the Emerald City before them. She wondered at the rapid flight of the Monkeys, but was glad the journey was over. The strange creatures set the travelers down carefully before the gate of the City, the King bowed low to Dorothy, and then flew swiftly away, followed by all his band.

"That was a good ride," said the little girl.

"Yes, and a quick way out of our troubles," replied the Lioness. "Well done for finding that wonderful Cap!"

Chapter XV

The Discovery of Oz, the Terrible

The four travelers walked up to the great gate of Emerald City and rang the bell. After ringing several times, it was opened by the same Guardian of the Gates they had met before.

"What! Are you back again?" he asked, in surprise.

"Do you not see us?" answered the Scarecrow.

"But I thought you had gone to visit the Wicked Witch of the West."

"We did visit her," said the Scarecrow.

"And she let you go again?" asked the man, in wonder.

"She could not help it, for she is melted," explained the Scarecrow.

"Melted! Well, that is good news, indeed," said the man. "Who melted her?"

"It was Dorothy," said the Lioness gravely.

"Good gracious!" exclaimed the man, and he bowed very low indeed before her.

Then he led them into his little room and locked the spectacles from the great box on all their eyes, just as he had done before. Afterward they passed on through the gate into the Emerald City.

When the people heard from the Guardian of the Gates that Dorothy had melted the Wicked Witch of the West, they all gathered around the travelers and followed them in a great crowd to the Palace of Oz.

The soldier with the green whiskers was still on guard before the door, but he let them in at once, and they were again met by the beautiful green girl, who showed each of them to their old rooms at once, so they might rest until the Great Oz was ready to receive them.

The soldier had the news carried straight to Oz that Dorothy and the other travelers had come back again, after destroying the Wicked Witch; but Oz made no reply.

The adventurers thought the Great Wizard would send for them at once, but he did not. They had no word from him the next day, nor the next, nor the next. The waiting was tiresome and wearing, and at last they grew vexed that Oz should treat them in so poor a fashion, after sending them to undergo hardships and slavery. So the Scarecrow at last asked the green girl to take another message to Oz, saying if he did not let them in to see him at once they would call the Winged Monkeys to help them, and find out whether he kept his promises or not.

When the Wizard was given this message he was so frightened that he sent word for them to come to the Throne Room at four minutes after nine o'clock the next morning. He had once met the Winged Monkeys in the Land of the West, and he did not wish to meet them again.

The four travelers passed a sleepless night, each thinking of the gift Oz had promised to bestow on him. Dorothy fell asleep only once, and then she dreamed she was in Kansas, where Aunt Em was telling her how glad she was to have her little girl at home again.

Promptly at nine o'clock the next morning the green-whiskered soldier came to them, and four minutes later they all went into the Throne Room of the Great Oz.

Of course each one of them expected to see the Wizard in the shape he had taken before, and all were greatly surprised when they looked about and saw no one at all in the room. They kept close to the door and closer to one another, for the stillness of the empty room was more dreadful than any of the forms they had seen Oz take.

Presently they heard a solemn Voice, that seemed to come from somewhere near the top of the great dome, and it said:

"I am Oz, the Great and Terrible. Why do you seek me?"

They looked again in every part of the room, and then, seeing no one, Dorothy asked, "Where are you?"

"I am everywhere," answered the Voice, "but to the eyes of common mortals I am invisible. I will now seat myself upon my throne, that you may converse with me." Indeed, the Voice seemed just then to come straight from the throne itself; so they walked toward it and stood in a row while Dorothy said:

"We have come to claim our promise, O Oz."

"What promise?" asked Oz.

"You promised to *Teleport* me back to Kansas when the Wicked Witch was destroyed," said the girl.

"And you promised to give me Intelligence," said the Scarecrow.

"And you promised to give me an *Atonement*," said the Tin Woman.

"And you promised to give me Rage," said the Cowardly Lioness.

"Is the Wicked Witch really destroyed?" asked the Voice, and Dorothy thought it trembled a little.

"Yes," she answered, "I melted her with a cup of quicksilver."

"Dear me," said the Voice, "how sudden! Well, come to me tomorrow, for I must have time to think it over."

"You've had plenty of time already," said the Tin Woman angrily.

"We shan't wait a day longer," said the Scarecrow.

"You must keep your promises to us!" exclaimed Dorothy.

The Lioness thought it might be as well to frighten the Wizard, so she gave a large, loud roar, which was so fierce and dreadful that Toto jumped away from her in alarm and tipped over the screen that stood in a corner. As it fell with a crash they looked that way, and the next moment all of them were filled with wonder. For they saw, standing in just the spot the screen had hidden, a little old man, with a bald head and a wrinkled face, who seemed to be as much surprised as they were. The Tin Woman, raising

137

her axe, rushed toward the little man and cried out, "Who are you?"

"I am Oz, the Great and Terrible," said the little man, in a trembling voice. "But don't strike me—please don't—and I'll do anything you want me to."

Our friends looked at him in surprise and dismay.

"I thought Oz was a great Head," said Dorothy.

"And I thought Oz was a lovely Lady," said the Scarecrow.

"And I thought Oz was a terrible Beast," said the Tin Woman.

"And I thought Oz was a Ball of Fire," exclaimed the Lioness.

"No, you are all wrong," said the little man meekly. "I have been making illusions."

"Making illusions!" cried Dorothy. "Are you not a Great Wizard of level fifteen?"

"Hush, my dear," he said. "Don't speak so loud, or you will be overheard—and I should be ruined. I'm supposed to be a Great Wizard."

"And aren't you?" she asked.

"Not a bit of it, my dear; I'm just a fifth level Illusionist."

"You're more than that," said the Scarecrow, in a grieved tone; "you're a humbug."

"Exactly so!" declared the little man, rubbing his hands together as if it pleased him. "I am a humbug."

"But this is terrible," said the Tin Woman. "How shall I ever get my *Atonement*?"

"Or I my *Rage*?" asked the Lioness.

"Or I my Intelligence?" wailed the Scarecrow, wiping the tears from his eyes with his coat sleeve.

"My dear friends," said Oz, "I pray you not to speak of these little things. Think of me, and the terrible trouble I'm in at being found out."

"Doesn't anyone else know you're a humbug?" asked Dorothy.

"No one knows it but you four—and myself," replied Oz. "I have fooled everyone so long that I thought I should never be found out. It was a great mistake my ever letting you into the Throne Room. Usually I will not see even my subjects, and so they believe I am something terrible."

"But, I don't understand," said Dorothy, in bewilderment. "How was it that you appeared to me as a great Head?"

"That was just an *Audible Force*," answered Oz. "Step this way, please, and I will tell you all about it."

He led the way to a small chamber in the rear of the Throne Room, and they all followed him. He pointed to one corner, in which lay the great Head, made out of many thicknesses of paper, and with a carefully painted face.

"This I hung from the ceiling by a wire," said Oz. "I stood behind the screen and pulled a thread, to make the eyes move and the mouth open."

"But how about the voice?" she inquired.

"Oh, that's where the *Audible Force* comes in," said the little man. "Using it, I can throw the sound of my voice wherever I wish and at great volume, so that you thought it was coming out of the

Head. Here are the other things I used to deceive you." He showed the Scarecrow the dress and the mask he had worn when he seemed to be the lovely Lady. And the Tin Woman saw that his terrible Beast was nothing but a lot of skins, sewn together, with slats to keep their sides out. As for the Ball of Fire, the false Wizard had hung that also from the ceiling. It was really a ball of cotton, but when oil was poured upon it the ball burned fiercely.

"Really," said the Scarecrow, "you ought to be ashamed of yourself for being such a humbug."

"I am—I certainly am," answered the little man sorrowfully; "but it was the only thing I could do. Sit down, please, there are plenty of chairs; and I will tell you my story."

So they sat down and listened while he told the following tale.

"I was born in Omaha—"

"Why, that isn't very far from Kansas!" cried Dorothy.

"No, but it's farther from here," he said, shaking his head at her sadly. "When I grew up I became an Illusionist, and at that I was very well trained by a great master who specialized in audible illusions. I can imitate any kind of a bird or beast." Here he mewed so like a kitten that Toto pricked up his ears and looked everywhere to see where she was. "After a time," continued Oz, "I tired of being stuck on level 1, and became a balloonist."

"What is that?" asked Dorothy.

"A man who goes up in a balloon on circus day, so as to draw a crowd of people together and get them to pay to see the circus," he explained. "By entertaining the crowds with my illusions cast from the balloon and grinding on repetitive carry and fetch quests I eventually gained enough experience to reach level five."

"Oh," she said, "I see."

"Well, one day I went up in a balloon and the ropes got twisted, so that I couldn't come down again. It went way up above the clouds, so far that a current of air struck it and carried it many, many miles away. For a day and a night I traveled through the air, and on the morning of the second day I awoke and found the balloon floating over a strange and beautiful country.

"It came down gradually, and I was not hurt a bit. But I found myself in the midst of a strange people, who, seeing me come from the clouds, thought I was a great Wizard. Of course I let them think so, because they were afraid of me, and promised to do anything I wished them to.

"Just to amuse myself, and keep the good people busy, I ordered them to build this City, and my Palace; and they did it all willingly and well. Then I thought, as the country was so green and beautiful, I would call it the Emerald City; and to make the name fit better I put green spectacles on all the people, so that everything they saw was green."

"But isn't everything here green?" asked Dorothy.

"No more than in any other city," replied Oz; "but when you wear green spectacles, why of course everything you see looks green to you. The Emerald City was built a great many years ago, for I was a young man when the balloon brought me here, and I am a very old man now. But my people have worn green glasses on their eyes so long that most of them think it really is an Emerald City, and it certainly is a beautiful place, abounding in jewels and precious metals, and every good thing that is needed to make one happy. I have been good to the people, and they like me; but ever since this Palace was built, I have shut myself up and would not see any of them.

"One of my greatest fears was the Witches, for while I had only the few spells of a level five Illusionist, I soon found out that the Witches were really able to do wonderful things. There were four of them in this country, and they ruled the people who live in the North and South and East and West. Fortunately, the Witches of the North and South were good, and I knew they would do me no harm; but the Witches of the East and West were terribly wicked, and had they not thought I was more powerful than they themselves, they would surely have destroyed me. As it was, I lived in deadly fear of them for many years; so you can imagine how pleased I was when I heard your house had fallen on the Wicked Witch of the East. When you came to me, I was willing to promise anything if you would only do away with the other Witch; but, now that you have melted her, I am ashamed to say that I cannot keep my promises."

"I think you are a very bad man: Chaotic Neutral bordering on Chaotic Evil," said Dorothy crossly.

"Oh, no, my dear; I'm really a very good man, but I'm a very bad Wizard, I must admit."

"Can't you give me Intelligence?" asked the Scarecrow.

"Do you really want your Bardic abilities restored? You are doing perfectly well without them."

"That may be true," said the Scarecrow, "but I shall be very unhappy unless you give me my Intelligence back."

The false Wizard looked at him carefully.

"Well," he said with a sigh, "I'm not much of a magician, as I said; but if you will come to me tomorrow morning, I will stuff your head with brains."

"Oh, thank you, thank you!" cried the Scarecrow. "I'll find a way to use them, never fear!"

"But how about my Rage?" asked the Lioness anxiously.

"You have plenty of other class features, I am sure," answered Oz. "All you need is confidence in yourself. There is no living thing that is not afraid when it faces danger. The true courage is in facing danger when you are afraid, and that kind of courage you have in plenty."

"Perhaps I have, but I'm restricted just the same," said the Lioness. "I shall really be very unhappy unless you give me Rage with all the benefits in morale, attack bonuses and resistances to mental attacks that come with it."

"Very well, I will give you Rage tomorrow," replied Oz.

"How about my *Atonement*?" asked the Tin Woman.

"Why, as for that," answered Oz, "I think you are wrong to want to be a Paladin. Following the Code of Conduct just makes most characters unhappy and stops them killing NPCs for experience. If you only knew it, you are in luck to be a Warrior and behave however you wish."

"That must be a matter of opinion," said the Tin Woman. "For my part, I will bear all the unhappiness without a murmur, if you will give me the *Atonement*."

"Very well," answered Oz meekly. "Come to me tomorrow and you shall have an *Atonement*. I have played Wizard for so many years that I may as well continue the part a little longer."

"And now," said Dorothy, "how am I to get back to Kansas?"

"We shall have to think about that," replied the little man. "Give me two or three days to consider the matter and I'll try to find a way to carry you over the desert. In the meantime you shall all be treated as my guests, and while you live in the Palace my people will wait upon you and obey your slightest wish. There is only one thing I ask in return for my help—such as it is. You must keep my secret and tell no one I am a humbug."

They agreed to say nothing of what they had learned, and went back to their rooms in high spirits. Even Dorothy had hope that "The Great and Terrible Humbug," as she called him, would find a way to send her back to Kansas, and if he did she was willing to forgive him everything.

CHAPTER XVI

The Magic Art of the Great Humbug

Next morning the Scarecrow said to his friends:

"Congratulate me. I am going to Oz to get my Intelligence at last. When I return I shall be as other Bards are."

"I have always liked you as you were," said Dorothy simply.

"It is kind of you to like a Scarecrow without the ability to give morale and other buffs," he replied. "But surely you will think more of me when you hear the splendid performances of my new Bardic abilities." Then he said good-bye to them all in a cheerful voice and went to the Throne Room, where he rapped upon the door.

"Come in," said Oz.

The Scarecrow went in and found the little man sitting down by the window, engaged in deep thought.

"I have come for my Intelligence," remarked the Scarecrow, a little uneasily.

"Oh, yes; sit down in that chair, please," replied Oz. "You must excuse me for taking your head off, but I shall have to do it in order to put your new brains in their proper place."

"That's all right," said the Scarecrow. "You are quite welcome to take my head off, as long as it will be a better one when you put it on again."

So the Wizard unfastened his head and emptied out the straw. Then he entered the back room and took up a measure of bran, which he mixed with half a potion of *Restoration*. Having shaken them together thoroughly, he filled the top of the Scarecrow's head with the mixture and stuffed the rest of the space with straw, with a Circlet of +4 Intelligence sewn on tightly to hold it in place.

When he had fastened the Scarecrow's head on his body again he said to him, "Hereafter you will be a great Bard, for I have given you your seven intelligence back, plus four more from the highest Intelligence item available in the city. But tell me, do you want to have the *Polymorph* dispelled and be restored to a human body?"

"I have thought long on this," replied Scarecrow, "and I like this body. I need not breathe. I need not eat. I need not fear falling. And even when my straw is scattered, I can be reassembled. There are a lot of exploits that become possible to me as a Straw man. It seems to me to be ideal."

The Scarecrow was both pleased and proud at the fulfilment of his greatest wish, and having thanked Oz warmly he went back to his friends.

Dorothy looked at him curiously. His head was quite bulged out at the top with the new mixture.

"How do you feel?" she asked.

"I feel Intelligent indeed," he answered earnestly. "When I get used to it, I shall cast spells and increase my skills and give twelve minutes of Bardic performance a day."

"Why is that circlet sewn onto your head?" asked the Tin Woman.

"So he can never lose it I suppose," remarked the Lioness.

"Well, I must go to Oz and get my *Atonement*," said the Tin Woman. So she walked to the Throne Room and knocked at the door.

"Come in," called Oz, and the Tin Woman entered and said, "I have come for my *Atonement*."

"Very well," answered the little man. "As you know, I am not a divine caster, but I have consulted with the highest level Lawful Good characters in the city, who believe the Goddess of Light will look favorably upon you and intervene if you make your pledge directly to her. Do you wish to proceed, knowing you will ever after honor her Code of Conduct?"

"Oh, yes," answered the Tin Woman. "I have felt lost without it."

So Oz brought the silver statue of the Goddess of Light and placed it on the table in front of the Tin Woman. Then, going to a chest of drawers, he took out a pretty gem in a golden circle, it span, sending colored rays of light around the room.

"Isn't it a beauty?" he asked.

"It is, indeed!" replied the Tin Woman, who was greatly pleased. "But what is it?"

147

"A Holy Symbol for the goddess," answered Oz. He set the gem turning. "Now place your hand over your heart and recall your brave deeds and repeat after me: I swear to uphold the Paladin's Code of Conduct with all my heart for all my days, however long that may be."

"I swear," said the Tin Woman solemnly, "to uphold the Paladin's Code of Conduct with all my heart for all my days, however long that may be."

The gem slowed and reached the limit of its turning in a clockwise direction, but before twisting back it held in place for a moment, casting golden light over the Tin Woman.

"There," said Oz; "did it work? Check your UI."

"Oh indeed," exclaimed the happy Tin Woman. "I am level seven Paladin—close to eight—with all my spells and bonuses restored! I am very grateful to you, and shall never forget your kindness."

"Don't speak of it," replied Oz.

Then the Tin Woman went back to her friends, who wished her every joy on account of her good fortune.

The Lioness now walked to the Throne Room and knocked at the door.

"Come in," said Oz.

"I have come for my Rage," announced the Lioness, entering the room.

"Very well," answered the little man; "I will get it for you."

He went to a cupboard and, reaching up to a high shelf, took down a square green bottle, the contents of which he poured into a green-gold dish, beautifully carved. Placing this before the Cowardly Lioness, who sniffed at it as if she did not like it, the Wizard said:

"Drink."

"What is it?" asked the Lioness.

"Well," answered Oz, "it is the rest of the potion of *Restoration* that I gave to Scarecrow."

The Lioness hesitated no longer, but drank till the dish was empty.

"How do you feel now?" asked Oz. "Is your Rage gem grayed out still?"

"It is green!" replied the Lioness, who went joyfully back to her friends to tell them of her good fortune.

Oz, left to himself, smiled to think of his success in giving the Scarecrow and the Tin Woman and the Lioness exactly what they thought they wanted. "Well, the people of the Emerald City were willing to give me the potion, the circlet and the advice about how to address the goddess. But no one had any idea about how to carry Dorothy back to Kansas, that will have to fall to me alone."

CHAPTER XVII

How the Balloon Was Launched

For three days Dorothy heard nothing from Oz. These were sad days for the little girl, although her friends were all quite happy and contented. The Scarecrow told them there were wonderful songs in his head; but he would not say what they were because he knew no one could understand them but himself. When the Tin Woman walked about she felt her love of the Munchkin returning; and she told Dorothy she had discovered it to be a kinder and more tender feeling than the one she had experienced when she was made of flesh. The Lioness declared she was afraid of nothing on earth, and with the benefits of Rage would gladly face an army or a dozen of the fierce Kalidahs.

Thus each of the little party was satisfied except Dorothy, who longed more than ever to get back to Kansas.

On the fourth day, to her great joy, Oz sent for her, and when she entered the Throne Room he greeted her pleasantly:

"Sit down, my dear; I think I have found the way to get you out of this country."

"And back to Kansas?" she asked eagerly.

"Well, I'm not sure about Kansas," said Oz, "for I haven't the faintest notion which way it lies. But the first thing to do is to cross the desert, and then it should be easy to find your way home."

"How can I cross the desert?" she inquired.

"Well, I'll tell you what I think," said the little man. "You see, when I came to this country it was in a balloon. You also came through the air, being carried by a cyclone. So I believe the best way to get across the desert will be through the air. Now, it is quite beyond my powers to make a cyclone; but I've been thinking the matter over, and I believe I can make a balloon."

"How?" asked Dorothy.

"A balloon," said Oz, "is made of silk, which is coated with glue to keep the gas in it. I have plenty of silk in the Palace, so it will be no trouble to make the balloon. But in all this country there is no gas to fill the balloon with, to make it float."

"If it won't float," remarked Dorothy, "it will be of no use to us."

"True," answered Oz. "But there is another way to make it float, which is to fill it with hot air. Hot air isn't as good as gas, for if the air should get cold the balloon would come down in the desert, and we should be lost."

"We!" exclaimed the girl. "Are you going with me?"

"Yes, of course," replied Oz. "I am tired of being such a humbug. If I should go out of this Palace my people would soon discover I am not a level fifteen Wizard, and then they would be vexed with me for having deceived them. So I have to stay shut up

151

in these rooms all day, and it gets tiresome. I'd much rather go back to Kansas with you and be in a circus again."

"I shall be glad to have your company," said Dorothy.

"Thank you," he answered. "Now, if you will help me sew the silk together, we will begin to work on our balloon."

So Dorothy took a needle and thread, and casting Haste found that as fast as Oz cut the strips of silk into proper shape she could sew them neatly together. First there was a strip of light green silk, then a strip of dark green and then a strip of emerald green; for Oz had a fancy to make the balloon in different shades of the color about them. It took three days to sew all the strips together, but when it was finished they had a big bag of green silk more than twenty feet long.

Then Oz painted it on the inside with a coat of thin glue, to make it airtight, after which he announced that the balloon was ready.

"But we must have a basket to ride in," he said. So he sent the soldier with the green whiskers for a big clothes basket, which he fastened with many ropes to the bottom of the balloon.

When it was all ready, Oz sent word to his people that he was going to make a visit to a great brother Wizard who lived in the clouds. The news spread rapidly throughout the city and everyone came to see the wonderful sight.

Oz ordered the balloon to be carried out in front of the Palace, and the people gazed upon it with much curiosity. The Tin Woman had chopped a big pile of wood, and now he made a fire of it, and Oz held the bottom of the balloon over the fire so that the hot air that arose from it would be caught in the silken bag. Gradually the balloon swelled out and rose into the air, until finally the basket just touched the ground.

Then Oz got into the basket and said to all the people in a loud voice:

"I am now going away to make a visit. While I am gone the Scarecrow will rule over you. I command you to obey him as you would me."

The balloon was by this time tugging hard at the rope that held it to the ground, for the air within it was hot, and this made it so much lighter in weight than the air without that it pulled hard to rise into the sky.

"Come, Dorothy!" cried the Wizard. "Hurry up, or the balloon will fly away."

"I can't find Toto anywhere," replied Dorothy, who did not wish to leave her familiar behind. Toto had run into the crowd to bark at a kitten, and Dorothy at last found him. She picked him up and ran toward the balloon.

She was within a few steps of it, and Oz was holding out his hands to help her into the basket, when, crack! went the ropes, and the balloon rose into the air without her.

"Come back!" she screamed. "I want to go, too!"

"I can't come back, my dear," called Oz from the basket. "Good-bye!"

"Good-bye!" shouted everyone, and all eyes were turned upward to where the Wizard was riding in the basket, rising every moment farther and farther into the sky.

And that was the last any of them ever saw of Oz, the Wonderful Wizard, though he may have reached Omaha safely, and be there now, for all we know. But the people remembered him lovingly, and said to one another:

"Oz was always our friend. When he was here he built for us this beautiful Emerald City, and now he is gone he has left the Wise Scarecrow to rule over us."

Still, for many days they grieved over the loss of the Wonderful Wizard, and would not be comforted.

Chapter XVIII

Away to the South

Dorothy wept bitterly at the passing of her hope to get home to Kansas again; but when she thought it all over she was glad she had not gone up in a balloon. And she also felt sorry at losing Oz, and so did her companions.

The Tin Woman came to her and said:

"Truly I should be ungrateful if I failed to mourn for the man who guided me in restoring me to my Code of Conduct. I should like to cry a little because Oz is gone, if you will kindly wipe away my tears, so that I shall not rust."

"With pleasure," she answered, and brought a towel at once. Then the Tin Woman wept for several minutes, and Dorothy watched the tears carefully and wiped them away with the towel. When the Tin Woman had finished, she thanked Dorothy kindly and oiled herself thoroughly with her jeweled oil-can, to guard against mishap.

The Scarecrow was now the ruler of the Emerald City, and although he was not a Wizard the people were proud of him. "For," they said, "there is not another city in all the world that is ruled by a stuffed Bard." And, so far as they knew, they were quite right.

The morning after the balloon had gone up with Oz, the four travelers met in the Throne Room and talked matters over. The Scarecrow sat in the big throne and the others stood respectfully before him.

"We are not so unlucky," said the new ruler, "for this Palace and the Emerald City belong to us, and we can do just as we please. When I remember that a short time ago I was up on a pole in a farmer's cornfield, and that now I am the ruler of this beautiful City, I am quite satisfied with my lot."

"I also," said the Tin Woman, "am well pleased with my being a Paladin again; and, really, that was the only thing I wished for in all the world."

"For my part, I am content in knowing I am as brave as any beast that ever lived, if not braver," said the Lioness modestly.

"If Dorothy would only be contented to live in the Emerald City," continued the Scarecrow, "we might all be happy together. Not to mention, go on adventures together."

"But I don't want to live here," cried Dorothy. "I want to go to Kansas, and help Aunt Em and Uncle Henry now I have such powerful magic."

"Well, then, what can be done?" inquired the Tin Woman.

The Scarecrow decided to think, and he thought so hard that the threads around his circlet began to strain. Finally he said:

"Why not call the Winged Monkeys, and ask them to carry you over the desert?"

"I never thought of that!" said Dorothy joyfully. "It's just the thing. I'll go at once for the Golden Cap."

When she brought it into the Throne Room she spoke the magic words, and soon the band of Winged Monkeys flew in through the open window and stood beside her.

"This is the second time you have called us," said the Monkey King, bowing before the little girl. "What do you wish?"

"I want you to fly with me to Kansas," said Dorothy.

But the Monkey King shook his head.

"That cannot be done," he said. "We belong to this country alone, and cannot leave it. There has never been a Winged Monkey in Kansas yet, and I suppose there never will be, for they don't belong there. We shall be glad to serve you in any way in our power, but we cannot cross the desert. Good-bye."

And with another bow, the Monkey King spread his wings and flew away through the window, followed by all his band.

Dorothy was ready to cry with disappointment. "I have wasted the charm of the Golden Cap to no purpose," she said, "for the Winged Monkeys cannot help me."

"It is certainly too bad!" said the tender-hearted Tin Woman.

The Scarecrow was thinking again, and his head bulged out so horribly that Dorothy feared it would burst.

"Let us call in the soldier with the green whiskers," he said, "and ask his advice."

So the soldier was summoned and entered the Throne Room timidly, for while Oz was alive he never was allowed to come farther than the door.

"This little girl," said the Scarecrow to the soldier, "wishes to cross the desert. How can she do so?"

"I cannot tell," answered the soldier, "for nobody has ever crossed the desert, unless it is Oz himself."

"Is there no one who can help me?" asked Dorothy earnestly.

"Glinda might," he suggested.

"Who is Glinda?" inquired the Scarecrow.

"The Witch of the South. She is the most powerful of all the Witches, and rules over the Quadlings. Besides, her castle stands on the edge of the desert, so she may know a way to cross it."

"Glinda is a Lawful Good Witch, isn't she?" asked the child.

"The Quadlings think she is Neutral Good," said the soldier, "and she is kind to everyone. Mind you, I have heard that Glinda is a beautiful woman, who knows how to keep young in spite of the many years she has lived."

"Could she be a vampire?" wondered the Tin Woman, fingering her axe.

"Oh, no," said the soldier. "For she has no fear of daylight."

"How can I get to her castle?" asked Dorothy.

"The road is straight to the South," he answered, "but it is said to be full of high-level wandering monsters and dangers to travelers. There are wild beasts in the woods, and a race of queer men

158

who do not like strangers to cross their country. For this reason none of the Quadlings ever come to the Emerald City."

The soldier then left them and the Scarecrow said:

"It seems, in spite of dangers, that the best thing Dorothy can do is to travel to the Land of the South and ask Glinda to help her. For, of course, if Dorothy stays here she will never get back to Kansas."

"You must have been thinking again," remarked the Tin Woman.

"I have," said the Scarecrow.

"I shall go with Dorothy," declared the Lioness, "for I am tired of your city and long for the woods and the country again. I am really a Barbarian, you know. Besides, Dorothy will need someone to protect her." She turned to Dorothy. "You have my two claws and a bite: with a leap attack of four claws and a bite once a day."

The Tin Woman spoke next, "And you have my axe! I will go with you to the Land of the South. Then I shall find my lost Munchkin and see if he still loves me."

"When shall we start?" asked the Scarecrow.

"Are you going?" they asked, in surprise.

"Certainly. If it wasn't for Dorothy I should never have my Bard abilities back. She lifted me from the pole in the cornfield and brought me to the Emerald City. So my good luck is all due to her, and I shall never leave her until she starts back to Kansas for good and all."

"Thank you," said Dorothy gratefully. "You are all very kind to me. But I should like to start as soon as possible."

"We shall go tomorrow morning," returned the Scarecrow. "So now let us all get ready, for it will be a long journey and although we are a strong party, we lack a healer."

CHAPTER XIX

Attacked by the Fighting Trees

The next morning Dorothy kissed the pretty green girl good-bye, and they all shook hands with the soldier with the green whiskers, who had walked with them as far as the gate. When the Guardian of the Gate saw them again he wondered greatly that they could leave the beautiful City to get into new trouble. But he at once unlocked their spectacles, which he put back into the green box, and gave them many good wishes to carry with them.

"You are now our ruler," he said to the Scarecrow; "so you must come back to us as soon as possible."

"I certainly shall if I am able," the Scarecrow replied; "but I must help Dorothy to get home, first."

As Dorothy bade the good-natured Guardian a last farewell she said:

"I have been very kindly treated in your lovely City, and every-one has been good to me. I cannot tell you how grateful I am."

"Don't try, my dear," he answered. "We should like to keep you with us, but if it is your wish to return to Kansas, I hope you will find a way." He then opened the gate of the outer wall, and they walked forth and started upon their journey.

The sun shone brightly as our friends turned their faces toward the Land of the South. They were all in the best of spirits, and laughed and chatted together. Dorothy was once more filled with the hope of getting home, and the Scarecrow and the Tin Woman were glad to be of use to her. As for the Lioness, she sniffed the fresh air with delight and whisked her tail from side to side in pure joy at being in the country again, while Toto ran around them and chased the moths and butterflies, barking merrily all the time.

"City life does not agree with me at all," remarked the Lioness, as they walked along at a brisk pace. "I have lost much flesh since I lived there, and now I am anxious for a chance to show the other beasts how courageous I have grown."

They now turned and took a last look at the Emerald City. All they could see was a mass of towers and steeples behind the green walls, and high up above everything the spires and dome of the Palace of Oz.

"Oz was not such a bad Wizard, after all," said the Tin Woman, as she felt her feeling of love grow.

"He knew how to give me Intelligence, and a score of eleven, too," said the Scarecrow.

"If Oz had the option to Rage like me," added the Lioness, "he would have been a brave man."

Dorothy said nothing. Oz had not kept the promise he made her, but he had done his best, so she forgave him. As he said, he was a good man, even if he was a bad Wizard.

The first day's journey was through the green fields and bright flowers that stretched about the Emerald City on every side. Knowing that this close to the Emerald City the random encounters were not dangerous, they slept that night on the grass, with nothing but the stars over them; and those who needed it rested very well indeed.

In the morning they traveled on until they came to a thick wood. There was no way of going around it, for it seemed to extend to the right and left as far as they could see; and, besides, they did not dare change the direction of their journey for fear of getting lost. So they looked for the place where it would be easiest to get into the forest.

The Scarecrow, who was in the lead, finally discovered a big tree with such wide-spreading branches that there was room for the party to pass underneath. So he walked forward to the tree, but just as he came under the first branches they bent down and twined around him, and the next minute he was raised from the ground and flung headlong among his fellow travelers.

This did not hurt the Scarecrow, but it surprised him, and he looked rather dizzy when Dorothy picked him up.

"Here is another space between the trees," called the Lioness.

"Let me try it first," said the Scarecrow, "for it doesn't hurt me to get thrown about." He walked up to another tree, as he spoke, but its branches immediately seized him and tossed him back again.

"This is strange," exclaimed Dorothy. "What shall we do?"

"The trees seem to have made up their minds to fight us, and stop our journey," remarked the Lioness.

"I'd love to try my first *Fireball*," said Dorothy.

"I believe ents, or whatever they are, are made for me," said the Tin Woman, and shouldering her axe, she marched up to the first tree that had handled the Scarecrow so roughly. When a big branch bent down to seize her the Tin Woman chopped at it so fiercely that she cut it in two. At once the tree began shaking all its branches as if in pain, and the Tin Woman passed safely under it.

"Come on!" she shouted to the others. "Be quick!" They all ran forward and passed under the tree without injury, except Toto, who was caught by a small branch and shaken until he howled from the loss of 7 hit points. But the Tin Woman promptly chopped off the branch and set the little dog free.

The other trees of the forest did nothing to keep them back, so they made up their minds that only the first row of trees could bend down their branches, and that probably these were the policemen of the forest, and given the duty of keeping strangers out of it.

"I could *Fireball* them?" offered Dorothy.

The Tin Woman shook her head. "They cannot harm us now."

"But they are terribly evil and might harm others in the future," said Scarecrow. "And they might have treasure under those root systems."

The Tin Woman narrowed her eyes as she used one of her three daily *Detect Evil* abilities. "No…" she said after a pause. "No, they aren't evil. Just protecting the forest."

Somewhat disappointed, the four travelers walked with ease through the trees until they came to the farther edge of the wood. Then, to their surprise, they found before them a high wall which seemed to be made of white china. It was smooth, like the surface of a dish, and higher than their heads.

"What shall we do now?" asked Dorothy.

"I will make a ladder," said the Tin Woman, "for we certainly must climb over the wall."

CHAPTER XX

The Dainty China Country

While the Tin Woman was making a ladder from wood which she found in the forest Dorothy lay down and slept, for she was tired by the long walk. The Lioness also curled herself up to sleep and Toto lay beside her.

The Scarecrow watched the Tin Woman while she worked, and said to her:

"I cannot think why this wall is here, nor what it is made of."

"Rest your brains and do not worry about the wall," replied the Tin Woman. "When we have climbed over it, we shall know what is on the other side."

After a time the ladder was finished. It looked clumsy, but the Tin Woman was sure it was strong and would answer their purpose. The Scarecrow waked Dorothy and the Lioness and Toto, and told them that the ladder was ready. The Scarecrow climbed up the ladder first, but he was so awkward that Dorothy had to follow close behind and keep him from falling off. When he got his head over the top of the wall the Scarecrow said, "Oh, my!"

"Go on," exclaimed Dorothy.

So the Scarecrow climbed farther up and sat down on the top of the wall, and Dorothy put her head over and cried, "Oh, my!" just as the Scarecrow had done.

Then Toto came up, and immediately began to bark, but Dorothy made him be still.

The Lioness climbed the ladder next, and the Tin Woman came last; but both of them cried, "Oh, my!" as soon as they looked over the wall. When they were all sitting in a row on the top of the wall, they looked down and saw a strange sight.

Before them was a great stretch of country having a floor as smooth and shining and white as the bottom of a big platter. Scattered around were many houses made entirely of china and painted in the brightest colors. These houses were quite small, the biggest of them reaching only as high as Dorothy's waist. There were also pretty little barns, with china fences around them; and many cows and sheep and horses and pigs and chickens, all made of china, were standing about in groups.

But the strangest of all were the people who lived in this queer country. There were milkmaids and shepherdesses, with brightly colored bodices and golden spots all over their gowns; and princesses with most gorgeous frocks of silver and gold and purple; and shepherds dressed in knee breeches with pink and yellow and blue stripes down them, and golden buckles on their shoes; and princes with jeweled crowns upon their heads, wearing ermine robes and satin doublets; and funny clowns in ruffled gowns, with round red spots upon their cheeks and tall, pointed caps. And,

167

strangest of all, these people were all made of china, even to their clothes, and were so small that the tallest of them was no higher than Dorothy's knee.

No one did so much as look at the travelers at first, except one little purple china dog with an extra-large head, which came to the wall and barked at them in a tiny voice, afterwards running away again.

"How shall we get down?" asked Dorothy.

They found the ladder so heavy they could not pull it up, so the Scarecrow fell off the wall and the others jumped down upon him so that the hard floor would not hurt their feet. Of course they took pains not to land on his head and the hard circlet. When all were safely down they picked up the Scarecrow, whose body was quite flattened out, and patted his straw into shape again.

"We must cross this strange place in order to get to the other side," said Dorothy, "for it would be unwise for us to go any other way except due South."

They began walking through the country of the china people, and the first thing they came to was a china milkmaid milking a china cow. As they drew near, the cow suddenly gave a kick and kicked over the stool, the pail, and even the milkmaid herself, and all fell on the china ground with a great clatter.

Dorothy was shocked to see that the cow had broken her leg off, and that the pail was lying in several small pieces, while the poor milkmaid had a nick in her left elbow.

"There!" cried the milkmaid angrily. "See what you have done! My cow has broken her leg, and I must take her to the mender's shop and have it glued on again. What do you mean by coming here and frightening my cow?"

"I'm very sorry," returned Dorothy. "Please forgive us."

But the pretty milkmaid was much too vexed to make any answer. She picked up the leg sulkily and led her cow away, the poor animal limping on three legs. As she left them the milkmaid cast many reproachful glances over her shoulder at the clumsy strangers, holding her nicked elbow close to her side.

Dorothy was quite grieved at this mishap.

"We must be very careful here," said the kind-hearted Tin Woman, "or we may hurt these pretty little people so they will never get over it."

"I wonder if their jewelry is lootable or just painted on the china?" mused Scarecrow.

A little farther on Dorothy met a most beautifully dressed young Princess, who stopped short as she saw the strangers and started to run away.

Dorothy wanted to test Scarecrow's theory, so she ran after her. But the china girl cried out:

"Don't chase me! Don't chase me!"

She had such a frightened little voice that Dorothy stopped and said, "Why not?"

"Because," answered the Princess, also stopping, a safe distance away, "if I run I may fall down and break myself."

169

"But could you not be mended?" asked the girl.

"Oh, yes; but one is never so pretty after being mended, you know," replied the Princess.

"I suppose not," said Dorothy.

"Now there is Mr. Joker, one of our clowns," continued the china lady, "who is always trying to stand upon his head. He has broken himself so often that he is mended in a hundred places, and doesn't look at all pretty. Here he comes now, so you can see for yourself."

Indeed, a jolly little clown came walking toward them, and Dorothy could see that in spite of his pretty clothes of red and yellow and green he was completely covered with cracks, running every which way and showing plainly that he had been mended in many places.

The Clown put his hands in his pockets, and after puffing out his cheeks and nodding his head at them saucily, he said:

"My lady fair,

Why do you stare

At poor old Mr. Joker?

You're quite as stiff

And prim as if

You'd eaten up a poker!"

"Be quiet, sir!" said the Princess. "Can't you see these are strangers, and should be treated with respect?"

"Well, here's respect; though not what you might expect," declared the Clown, and immediately began waving his arms and muttering.

"Are you casting a spell?"

"What you say is true; I've just cast *Glue!*"

"Don't mind Mr. Joker," said the Princess to Dorothy. "He is considerably cracked in his head, and that makes him Chaotic Neutral."

"Oh," said Dorothy. "But it does seem as though he has stuck my feet to the ground."

"Mine too," said the Tin Woman.

"My paws are all stuck hard," added the Lioness.

"As are my shoes." Scarecrow lifted a straw leg out of his shoe.

Even Toto could not move and he began to bark.

"Oh dear," answered the china Princess. "You might have frightened him."

"Dear Mr. Joker," said Dorothy carefully, "please undo your spell. We don't mean any harm."

The Clown leaned forward and gave a knowing wink. "Player characters just want gold; NPCs rarely get to grow old. You can stay there all day, until Mr. Joker is safely away." With that he gave a skip and turned to leave.

A strum of a chord on a lute caused the Clown to stop.

"A Clown of china is a wonderful being…" sang Scarecrow, utilizing his Bardic performance for the first time since being *Cursed*.

Mr. Joker looked back over his shoulder.

"Whose clever tricks are well worth seeing…"

Mr. Joker turned back to face the party.

"His rhymes are fun; his rhymes are witty…"

Mr. Joker took a step towards them.

"And his friends of china are terribly pretty."

Mr. Joker looked at Scarecrow and his smile was genuine and warm. With a gesture, the Clown ended the *Glue* spell and the relieved party moved southwards.

"Good-bye Mr. Joker; goodbye Princess," said Dorothy.

"Good-bye," replied the Princess.

Mr. Joker doffed his hat.

They walked carefully away through the china country.

"What Bardic performance was that?" asked the Tin Woman.

"*Remove Fear.*" Scarecrow replied, placing his lute over his back once more. "It seemed that he wasn't really a hostile mob. And I don't think he had any loot. So I thought I'd act on the information the Princess gave us."

"Well done," said Dorothy and if Scarecrows could blush, this one did.

As they travelled, the little animals and all the people scampered out of their way, fearing the strangers would break them, and after an hour or so the travelers reached the other side of the country and came to another china wall.

It was not so high as the first, however, and by standing upon the Lioness's back they all managed to scramble to the top. Then the Lioness gathered her legs under her and jumped on the wall; but just as she jumped, she upset a china church with her tail and smashed it all to pieces.

"That was too bad," said Dorothy, "but really I think we were lucky in not doing these little people more harm than breaking a cow's leg and a church. They are all so brittle!"

"They are, indeed," said the Scarecrow, "and I am thankful I am made of straw and cannot be easily damaged. There are worse things in the world than being a Scarecrow."

CHAPTER XXI

The Lioness Becomes the Queen of Beasts

After climbing down from the china wall the travelers found themselves in a disagreeable country, full of bogs and marshes and covered with tall, rank grass. It was difficult to walk without falling into muddy holes, for the grass was so thick that it hid them from sight. By carefully picking their way, however, they got safely along until they reached solid ground. But here the country seemed wilder than ever, and after a long and tiresome walk through the underbrush they entered another forest, where the trees were bigger and older than any they had ever seen.

"This forest is perfectly delightful," declared the Lioness, looking around her with joy. "Never have I seen a more beautiful place."

"It seems gloomy," said the Scarecrow.

"Not a bit of it," answered the Lioness. "I should like to live here all my life. See how soft the dried leaves are under your feet and how rich and green the moss is that clings to these old trees. Surely no Barbarian could wish a pleasanter home."

"Perhaps there are wild beasts in the forest now," said Dorothy.

"I suppose there are," returned the Lioness, "but I do not see any of them about."

They walked through the forest until it became too dark to go any farther. Dorothy and Toto and the Lioness lay down to sleep, while the Tin Woman and the Scarecrow kept watch over them as usual.

When morning came, they started again. Before they had gone far they heard a low rumble, as of the growling of many wild animals. Toto whimpered a little, but none of the others were frightened, and they kept along the well-trodden path until they came to an opening in the wood, in which were gathered hundreds of beasts of every variety. There were tigers and elephants and bears and wolves and foxes and all the others in the natural history, and for a moment Dorothy was afraid. But the Lioness explained that the animals were holding a meeting, and she judged by their snarling and growling that they were in great trouble.

As she spoke several of the beasts caught sight of her, and at once the great assemblage hushed as if by magic. The biggest of the tigers came up to the Lioness and bowed, saying:

"Welcome, O Queen of Beasts! You have come in good time to fight our enemy and bring peace to all the animals of the forest once more."

"What is your trouble?" asked the Lioness quietly.

"We are all threatened," answered the tiger, "by a fierce enemy which has lately come into this forest. It is a most tremendous monster, like a great spider, with a body as big as an elephant and legs as long as a tree trunk. It has eight of these long legs, and as the monster crawls through the forest he seizes an animal with a leg and drags it to his mouth, where he eats it as a spider does a fly. Not one of us is safe while this fierce creature is alive, and we had called a meeting to decide how to take care of ourselves when you came among us."

The Lioness thought for a moment.

"Are there any other Lionesses in this forest?" she asked.

"No; there were some, but the monster has eaten them all. And, besides, they were none of them nearly so large and brave as you."

"If I put an end to your enemy, will you bow down to me and obey me as Queen of the Forest?" inquired the Lioness.

"We will do that gladly," returned the tiger; and all the other beasts roared with a mighty roar: "We will!"

"Where is this great spider of yours now?" asked the Lioness.

"Yonder, among the oak trees," said the tiger, pointing with his forefoot.

"Take good care of these friends of mine," said the Lioness, "and I will go at once to fight the monster."

"Oh no," said Dorothy, "we are coming with you."

"That's right," said the Tin Woman, hefting her axe. "Here's a truly evil monster that I can fight without violating my Code."

"Never split the party," added the Scarecrow. And even Toto ran ahead courageously.

The great spider was lying asleep when the party found him, and it looked so horrific that Dorothy took a step back in disgust. Its legs were quite as long as the tiger had said, and its body covered with coarse black hair. It had a great mouth, with a row of sharp teeth a foot long; but its head was joined to the pudgy body by a neck as slender as a wasp's waist. This gave the Lioness a hint of the best way to attack the creature.

"We should try to get a critical hit on the weak point."

"I'll focus my *Magic Missiles* there too," said Dorothy, edging just close enough that she could target the monster. Next, she cast *Haste* on them all, followed by *Summon Monster VI*, which brought a Giant Ape to her side. "Ready," she said.

The Lioness moved with a high Stealth skill toward the sleeping monster, but the Tin Woman and the Scarecrow both failed their checks, the cracking of twigs underfoot giving them away.

At once the spider leaped up, its many eyes shiny with anger, its mandibles clicking and its mouth dripping with venom. Rearing up and waving its front two legs, the effect was to create a *Fear* spell upon them all.

The Lioness triggered Rage and was immune to *Fear*, leaping forward with two claws and a bite. Brave Toto made his resist too. But Dorothy and Scarecrow both felt the need to sprint away as top speed, until the Tin Woman cried "Rally" and immediately they felt calmer.

The hit point bar of the giant spider began to drop, but not as alarmingly as that of the Lioness.

"We need the Tin Woman to be tank," shouted Scarecrow, "we don't have a healer."

While Dorothy's pet Ape was hurling rocks at the monster and Toto was courageously running around trying to bite its legs, she repeatedly cast *Magic Missile*, draining her mana bar.

"Back away, Lioness," urged the Tin Woman.

But Lioness was Raging for the first time in weeks and would never cease her attacks so long as she could draw breath or the Spider was dead.

As it was impossible to shift the aggro to anyone else, the battle became a race to lower the monster's hit points before it killed Lioness. Everyone gave their utmost but what tipped the balance was Scarecrow's rediscovered Bardic abilities. Experienced Bards could 'twist' two performances around each other to create two simultaneous magical effects. Scarecrow managed to sing a healing song while drumming an inspiration that increased the rate of critical hits.

At last, with one savage blow of Lioness's heavy paw, all armed with sharp claws, she knocked the spider's upper torso from the lower. Jumping to pin down the head, she watched the monster until the long legs stopped wiggling, when she knew it was quite dead.

"Ding!" cried Dorothy delightedly. "I'm level ten."

"I've levelled up too," said Lioness, "I'm a level eight Barbarian."

"Level eight Paladin," said the Tin Woman.

"Level eight Bard," announced Scarecrow proudly.

With the exception of the summoned Giant Ape, who returned to the forest, they went back to the opening where the beasts of the forest were waiting for her and Lioness said proudly:

"You need fear your enemy no longer."

Then the beasts bowed down to the Lioness as their Queen, and she promised to come back and rule over them as soon as Dorothy was safely on her way to Kansas.

CHAPTER **XXII**

The Country of the Quadlings

The four travelers passed through the rest of the forest in safety, and when they came out from its gloom saw before them a steep hill, covered from top to bottom with great pieces of rock.

"That will be a hard climb," said the Scarecrow, "but we must get over the hill, nevertheless."

So he led the way and the others followed. They had nearly reached the first rock when they heard a rough voice cry out, "Keep back!"

"Who are you?" asked the Scarecrow.

Then a head showed itself over the rock and the same voice said, "This hill belongs to us, and we don't allow anyone to cross it."

"But we must cross it," said the Scarecrow. "We're going to the country of the Quadlings."

"But you shall not!" replied the voice, and there stepped from behind the rock the strangest man the travelers had ever seen.

He was quite short and stout and had a big head, which was flat at the top and supported by a thick neck full of wrinkles. But he had no arms at all, and, seeing this, the Scarecrow did not fear that so helpless a creature could prevent them from climbing the hill. So he said, "I'm sorry not to do as you wish, but we must pass over your hill whether you like it or not," and he walked boldly forward.

As quick as lightning the man's head shot forward and his neck stretched out until the top of the head, where it was flat, struck the Scarecrow in the middle and sent him tumbling, over and over, down the hill. Almost as quickly as it came the head went back to the body, and the man laughed harshly as he said, "It isn't as easy as you think!"

A chorus of boisterous laughter came from the other rocks, and Dorothy saw hundreds of the armless Hammer-Heads upon the hillside, one behind every rock.

The Lioness became quite angry at the laughter caused by the Scarecrow's mishap, and giving a loud roar that echoed like thunder, she dashed up the hill.

Again a head shot swiftly out, and the great Lioness went rolling down the hill as if she had been struck by a cannon ball, suffering a noticeable drop to her hit point bar.

Dorothy ran down and helped the Scarecrow to his feet, and the Lioness came up to her, feeling rather bruised and sore, and said, "It is useless to fight people with shooting heads; no one can withstand them."

"What can we do, then?" she asked.

"Call the Winged Monkeys," suggested the Tin Woman. "You have still the right to command them once more."

181

"Very well," she answered, and putting on the Golden Cap she uttered the magic words. The Monkeys were as prompt as ever, and in a few moments the entire band stood before her.

"What are your commands?" inquired the King of the Monkeys, bowing low.

"Carry us over the hill to the country of the Quadlings," answered the girl.

"It shall be done," said the King, and at once the Winged Monkeys caught the four travelers and Toto up in their arms and flew away with them. As they passed over the hill the Hammer-Heads yelled with vexation, and shot their heads high in the air, but they could not reach the Winged Monkeys, who carried Dorothy and her comrades safely over the hill and set them down in the beautiful country of the Quadlings.

"This is the last time you can summon us," said the leader to Dorothy; "so good-bye and good luck to you."

"Good-bye, and thank you very much," returned the girl; and the Monkeys rose into the air and were out of sight in a twinkling.

"I wonder if there's an exploit here with the Golden Cap," mused Scarecrow. "You could give it to me and then I'd have three commands over the flying monkeys."

"Oh what a good idea," said Dorothy.

"It would break my Code," the Tin Woman pointed out. "Despite the fact that the Winged Monkeys nearly killed me, I cannot approve of taking advantage of their servitude." So the party continued on their journey.

182

The country of the Quadlings seemed rich and happy. There was field upon field of ripening grain, with well-paved roads running between, and pretty rippling brooks with strong bridges across them. The fences and houses and bridges were all painted bright red, just as they had been painted yellow in the country of the Winkies and blue in the country of the Munchkins. The Quadlings themselves, who were short and fat and looked chubby and good-natured, were dressed all in red, which showed bright against the green grass and the yellowing grain.

The Monkeys had set them down near a farmhouse, and the four travelers walked up to it and knocked at the door. It was opened by a female NPC farmer, and when Dorothy asked for something to eat the woman gave them all a good dinner, with three kinds of cake and four kinds of cookies, and a bowl of milk for Toto.

"How far is it to the Castle of Glinda?" asked the child.

"It is not a great way," answered the farmer's wife. "Take the road to the South and you will soon reach it."

Thanking the good woman, they started afresh and walked by the fields and across the pretty bridges until they saw before them a very beautiful Castle. Before the gates were three young girls, dressed in handsome red uniforms trimmed with gold braid; and as Dorothy approached, one of them said to her:

"Why have you come to the South Country?"

"To see the Good Witch who rules here," she answered. "Will you take me to her?"

183

"Let me have your name, and I will ask Glinda if she will receive you." They told who they were, and the girl soldier went into the Castle. After a few moments she came back to say that Dorothy and the others were to be admitted at once.

Chapter XXIII

Glinda The Good Witch Grants Dorothy's Wish

Before they went to see Glinda, however, they were taken to a room of the Castle, where Dorothy washed her face and combed her hair, and the Lioness shook the dust out of her coat of fur, and the Scarecrow patted himself into his best shape, and the Tin Woman polished her tin and oiled her joints.

When they were all quite presentable they followed the soldier girl into a big room where the Witch Glinda sat upon a throne of rubies.

She was both beautiful and young to their eyes. Her hair was a rich red in color and fell in flowing ringlets over her shoulders. Her dress was pure white but her eyes were blue, and they looked kindly upon the little girl.

"What can I do for you, my child?" she asked.

Dorothy told the Witch all her story: how the cyclone had brought her to the Land of Oz, how she had found her companions, and of the wonderful adventures they had met with.

"My greatest wish now," she added, "is to get back to Kansas, for Aunt Em will surely think something dreadful has happened to me, and that will make her put on mourning; and unless the crops are better this year than they were last, I am sure Uncle Henry cannot afford it. But now I am a level ten sorceress, I can be a great help."

Glinda leaned forward and kissed the sweet, upturned face of the loving little girl.

"Bless your dear heart," she said, "I am sure I can tell you of a way to get back to Kansas." Then she added, "But, if I do, you must give me the Golden Cap."

"Willingly!" exclaimed Dorothy; "indeed, it is of no use to me now, and when you have it you can command the Winged Monkeys three times."

"And I think I shall need their service just those three times," answered Glinda, smiling.

"I am not sure this is right," said the Tin Woman. "It's an exploit and keeps the Flying Monkeys in perpetual servitude."

"Allow me to explain." The Witch turned to the Scarecrow. "What will you do when Dorothy has left us?"

"I will return to the Emerald City," he replied, "for Oz has made me its ruler and the people like me. The only thing that worries me is how to cross the hill of the Hammer-Heads."

"By means of the Golden Cap I shall command the Winged Monkeys to carry you to the gates of the Emerald City," said

Glinda, "for it would be a shame to deprive the people of so wonderful a ruler."

"Am I really wonderful?" asked the Scarecrow.

"You are unusual," replied Glinda.

Turning to the Tin Woman, she asked, "What will become of you when Dorothy leaves this country?"

She leaned on her axe and thought a moment. Then she said, "Now that I am a Paladin once more and am filled with the joy of serving goodness, I find myself full of love for the young man whom I once abandoned. I shall return to him and if he will still have me, I will marry him. If not, I shall be sad but determined to make further amends by following the Code.

"Either way, I shall then rule over the Winkies and show them that a Lawful Good ruler makes for a far happier realm than a Chaotic Evil one."

"My second command to the Winged Monkeys," said Glinda "will be that they carry you safely to the youth you speak of and then to the land of the Winkies: alone or with him. Your brain may not be so large to look at as that of the Scarecrow, but you are really brighter than he is—when you are well polished—and I am sure you will rule the Winkies wisely and well."

Then the Witch looked at the big, shaggy Lioness and asked, "When Dorothy has returned to her own home, what will become of you?"

"Over the hill of the Hammer-Heads," she answered, "lies a grand old forest, and all the beasts that live there have made me their Queen. If I could only get back to this forest, I would pass my life very happily there."

"My third command to the Winged Monkeys," said Glinda, "shall be to carry you to your forest. Then, having used up the powers of the Golden Cap, I shall give it to the King of the Monkeys, that he and his band may thereafter be free for evermore. Is that acceptable to your Code, Tin Woman?"

"If the King of the Monkeys comes and you explain this plan and he agrees, then all will be good."

The Scarecrow and the Lioness now thanked the Good Witch earnestly for her kindness; and Dorothy exclaimed:

"You are certainly as good as you are beautiful! But you have not yet told me how to get back to Kansas."

"Your Silver Shoes will carry you over the desert," replied Glinda. "If you had known their power you could have gone back to your Aunt Em the very first day you came to this country."

"But then I should not have had my wonderful eleven Intelligence!" cried the Scarecrow. "I might have passed my whole life in the farmer's cornfield."

"And I should not have had my Paladin class restored," said the Tin Woman. "And I might have stood and rusted in the forest till the end of the world."

"And I should have lived without Rage forever," declared the Lioness, "and no beast in all the forest would have had a good word to say to me."

188

"This is all true," said Dorothy, "and I am glad I was of use to these good friends. But now that each of them has had what he or she most desired, and each is happy in having a kingdom to rule besides, I think I should like to go back to Kansas."

"The Silver Shoes," said the Good Witch, "have wonderful powers. And one of the most curious things about them is that they can carry you to any place in the world in three steps, and each step will be made in the wink of an eye. All you have to do is to knock the heels together three times and command the shoes to carry you wherever you wish to go."

"If that is so," said the child joyfully, "I will ask them to carry me back to Kansas at once."

Dorothy threw her arms around the Lioness's neck and kissed her, patting her big head tenderly. Then she kissed the Tin Woman, who was weeping in a way most dangerous to her joints. But she hugged the soft, stuffed body of the Scarecrow in her arms instead of kissing his painted face, and found she was crying herself at this sorrowful parting from her loving comrades.

Glinda the Good stepped down from her ruby throne to give the little girl a good-bye kiss, and Dorothy thanked her for all the kindness she had shown to her friends and herself.

Dorothy now took Toto up solemnly in her arms, and having said one last good-bye she clapped the heels of her shoes together three times, saying:

"Take me home to Aunt Em!"

Instantly she was whirling through the air, so swiftly that all she could see or feel was the wind whistling past her ears.

The Silver Shoes took but three steps, and then she stopped so suddenly that she rolled over upon the grass several times before she knew where she was.

At length, however, she sat up and looked about her.

"Good gracious!" she cried.

For she was sitting on the broad Kansas prairie, and just before her was the new farmhouse Uncle Henry built after the cyclone had carried away the old one. Uncle Henry was milking the cows in the barnyard, and Toto had jumped out of her arms and was running toward the barn, barking furiously.

CHAPTER XXIV

Home Again

Aunt Em had just come out of the house to water the cabbages when she looked up and saw Dorothy running toward her.

"My darling child!" she cried, folding the little girl in her arms and covering her face with kisses. "Where in the world did you come from?"

"From the Land of Oz," said Dorothy gravely. "And here is Toto, too. And oh, Aunt Em! I'm so glad to be at home again!"

Uncle Henry came forward, with a happy expression that Dorothy had never seen before.

"My dear; we thought you lost to the cyclone. Yet here you are, looking so well." He paused, looking at her with astonishment. "My, you are level ten!"

Dorothy laughed. "So I am, and dear Toto is level six."

With great pleasure, she took a long look at the character sheet on her UI. She had come a long way from the little girl with only one level in Sorceress:

Dorothy, level 10 Sorceress
HP 55   Mana 124

AC: 2 (clothes 0, +2 bracelet)

Str 7

Int 17

Wis 11

Con 7

Dex 7

Cha 13

Spell gem slots:

5 level 1 Spells

4 level 2 Spells

3 level 3 Spells

3 level 4 Spells

2 level 5 Spells

Silver Shoes of Proicio

ABOUT THE AUTHOR

Oisin Muldowney is a software engineer living in Galway, Ireland.

He'd be happy to hear from readers, please email: chatbotsireland@gmail.com, or message him on Reddit. https://www.reddit.com/user/OisinM

Oisin dips in and out of a number of LitRPG communities:
https://www.reddit.com/r/litrpg/
https://www.facebook.com/groups/LitRPGsociety
https://www.facebook.com/groups/LitRPGGroup
https://www.facebook.com/groups/LitRPGAdventures
https://www.facebook.com/groups/LitRPGForum
https://www.facebook.com/groups/LitRPG.books
https://www.facebook.com/groups/LitRPGAdventures/
https://www.facebook.com/groups/GameLitSociety
https://www.facebook.com/groups/181286032649395
https://www.facebook.com/litrpgreads

LEVEL UP PUBLISHING

Level Up publishing specialises in LitRPG and GameLit books. If you have enjoyed *The Wonderful* LitRPG *Wizard of Oz* you might be interested in our other titles, which can be found at www.levelup.pub/books

To join our mailing list for news about forthcoming books and opportunities to be an ARC reader, just fill in the form on that page.

You can also find us on:
Facebook @LUPublishing
Twitter @LevelUpPub